I0755679

POEMS

BY

CHARLES KINGSLEY,

AUTHOR OF "AMYAS LEIGH," "HYPATIA," &c.

SECOND EDITION.

BOSTON:
TICKNOR AND FIELDS.
MDCCCLVI.

RIVERSIDE, CAMBRIDGE:
STEREOTYPED AND PRINTED BY
H. O. HOUGHTON AND COMPANY.

AUTHOR'S EDITION.

CONTENTS.

MISCELLANEOUS POEMS.

BALLADS.

THE

SAINT'S TRAGEDY:

OR,

THE TRUE STORY OF ELIZABETH OF HUNGARY,

LANDGRAVINE OF THURINGIA,

SAINT OF THE ROMISH CALENDAR.

PREFACE

TO THE

SAINT'S TRAGEDY.

BY THE

REV. F. D. MAURICE, M.A.

THE writer of this play does not differ with his countrymen generally, as to the nature and requirements of a Drama. He has learnt from our Great Masters that it should exhibit human beings engaged in some earnest struggle, certain outward aspects of which may possibly be a spectacle for the amusement of idlers, but which in itself is for the study and sympathy of those who are struggling themselves. A Drama, he feels, should not aim at the inculcation of any definite maxim; the moral of it lies in the action and the character. It must be drawn out of them by the heart and experience of the reader, not forced upon him by the author. The men and women whom he presents are not to be his spokesmen; they are to utter themselves freely in such language, grave or mirthful, as best expresses what they feel and what they are. The age to which they belong is neither to be contemplated as if it were apart from us, nor is it to be measured by our rules, neither to be held up as a model, nor to be condemned for its strangeness. The passions which worked in it must be those which are working in ourselves. To the same eternal laws and principles are we, and it, amenable. By beholding these a poet is to raise himself, and may hope to raise his readers, above antiquarian tastes and modern conventions. The unity of the play cannot be conferred upon it by any artificial arrangements ; it must depend upon the relation of the different persons and events to the central subject. No nice adjustments of success and failure to right and wrong must constitute its poetical justice. In some deeper way than this, if at all, must the conscience of the readers be satisfied that there is an order in the universe, and that the poet has perceived and asserted it.

Long before these principles were reduced into formal canons of orthodoxy, even while they encountered the strong opposition of critics, they were unconsciously recognized by Englishmen as sound and national. Yet I question whether a clergyman, writing in conformity with them, might not have incurred censure in former times, and may not incur it now. The privilege of expressing his own thoughts, sufferings, sympathies, in any form of verse is easily conceded to him; if he liked to use a dialogue instead of a monologue, for the purpose of enforcing a duty, or illustrating a doctrine, no one would find fault with him; if he produced an actual Drama for the purpose of defending or denouncing a particular character, or period, or system of opinions, the compliments of one party might console him for the abuse or contempt of another.

But it seems to be supposed that he is bound to keep in view one or other of these ends: while to divest himself of his own individuality that he may enter into the working of other spirits; to lay aside the authority which pronounces one opinion, or one habit of mind, to be right and another wrong, that he may exhibit them in their actual strife; to deal with questions, not in an abstract shape, but mixed up with the affections, passions, relations of human creatures — is a course which must lead him, it is thought, into a great forgetfulness of his office, and of all that is involved in it.

No one can have less interest than I have in claiming poetical privileges for the clergy; and no one, I believe, is more thoroughly convinced that the standard which society prescribes for us, and to which we ordinarily conform ourselves, instead of being too severe and lofty, is far too secular and grovelling. But I apprehend the limitations of this kind which are imposed upon us are themselves exceedingly secular, betokening an entire misconception of the nature of our work, proceeding from maxims and habits which tend to make it utterly insignificant and abortive. If a man confines himself to the utterance of his own experiences, those experiences are likely to become every day more narrow and less real. If he confines himself to the defence of certain propositions, he is sure gradually to lose all sense of the connection between those propositions and his own life, or the life of man. In either case he becomes utterly ineffectual as a teacher. Those whose education and character are different from his own, whose processes of mind have therefore been different, are utterly unintelligible to him. Even a cordial desire for sympathy is not able to break through the prickly hedge of habits, notions, and technicalities, which separates them. Oftentimes the desire itself is extinguished in those who ought to cherish it most, by the fear of meeting with something portentous or dangerous. Nor can he defend a dogma better than he communes with men; for he knows not that which attacks it. He supposes it to be a set of book arguments, whereas it is something lying very deep in the heart of the disputant, into which he has never penetrated.

Hence there is a general complaint that we "are ignorant of the thoughts and feelings of our contemporaries;" most attribute this to a fear of looking below the surface, lest we should find hollowness within; many like to have it so, because they have thus an excuse for despising us. But surely such an ignorance is more inexcusable in us, than in the priests of any nation: we, less than any, are kept from the sun and air; our discipline is less than any contrived merely to make us acquainted with the commonplaces of divinity. We are enabled, nay, obliged, from our youth upwards, to mix with people of our own age, who are destined for all occupations and modes of life; to share in their studies, their enjoyments, their perplexities, their temptations. Experience, often so dearly bought, is surely not meant to be thrown away: whether it has been obtained without the sacrifice of that which is most precious, or whether the lost blessing has been restored twofold, and good is understood, not only as the opposite of evil, but as the deliverance from it, we cannot be meant to forget all that we have been learning. The teachers of other nations may reasonably mock us, as having less of direct book-lore than themselves; they should not be able to say, that we are without the compensation of knowing a little more of living creatures.

A clergyman, it seems to me, should be better able than other men to cast aside that which is merely accidental, either in his own character, or in the character of the age to which he belongs, and to apprehend that which is essential and eternal. His acceptance of fixed creeds, which belong as much to one generation as another, and which have survived amid all changes and convulsions, should raise him especially above the temptation to exalt the fashion of his own time, or of any past one; above the affectation of the obsolete, above slavery to the present, and above that strange mixture of both which some display, who weep because the beautiful visions of the Past are departed, and admire themselves for being able to weep over them — and dispense with them. His reverence for the Bible should make him feel that we most realize our own personality when we most connect it with that of our fellow-men; that acts are not to be contemplated apart from the actor; that more of what is acceptable to the God of Truth may come forth in men striving with infinite confusion and often uttering words like the east wind, than in those who can discourse calmly and eloquently about a righteousness and mercy which they know only by hearsay. The belief which a minister of God has in the eternity of the distinction between right and wrong should especially dispose him to recognize that distinction apart from mere circumstance and opinion. The confidence which he must have that the life of each man, and the life of this world, is a drama, in which a perfectly Good and True Being is unveiling His own purposes, and carrying on a conflict with evil, which must issue in complete victory, should make him eager to discover in every portion of history, in every biography, a divine "Morality" and "Mystery" — a morality, though it deals with no abstract personages — a mystery, though the subject of it be the doings of the most secular men.

The subject of this Play is certainly a dangerous one. It suggests questions which are deeply interesting at the present time. It involves the whole character and spirit of the Middle Ages. A person who had not an enthusiastic admiration for the character of Elizabeth would not be worthy to speak of her; it seems to me, that he would be still less worthy, if he did not admire far more fervently that ideal of the female character which God has established, and not man — which she imperfectly realized — which often exhibited itself in her in spite of her own more confused, though apparently more lofty ideal; which may be manifested more simply, and therefore more perfectly, in the England of the nineteenth century, than in the Germany of the thirteenth. To enter into the meaning of self-sacrifice — to sympathize with any one who aims at it — not to be misled by counterfeits of it — not to be unjust to the truth which may be mixed with those counterfeits — is a difficult task, but a necessary one for any one who takes this work in hand. How far our author has attained these ends, others must decide. I am sure that he will not have failed from forgetting them. He has, I believe, faithfully studied all the documents of the period within his reach, making little use of modern narratives; he has meditated upon the past in its connection with the present; has never allowed his reading to become dry by disconnecting it with what he has seen and felt, or made his partial experiences a measure for the acts which they help him to understand. He has entered upon his work at least in a true and faithful spirit, not regarding it as an amusement for leisure hours, but as something to be done seriously, if done at all; as if he was as much "under the Great Taskmaster's eye" in this as in any other duty of his calling. In certain passages and scenes he seemed to me to have been a little too bold for the taste and temper of this age. But having written them deliberately, from a conviction that morality is in peril from fastidiousness, and that it is not safe to look at questions which are really agitating people's hearts merely from the outside — he has, and I believe rightly, retained what I should, from cowardice, have wished him to exclude. I have no doubt, that any one who wins a victory over the fear of opinion, and especially over the opinion of the religious world, strengthens his own moral character, and acquires a greater fitness for his high service.

Whether Poetry is again to revive among us, or whether the power is to be wholly stifled by our accurate notions about the laws and conditions under which it is to be exercised, is a question upon which there is room for great differences of opinion. Judging from the past, I should suppose that till Poetry becomes less self-conscious, less self-concentrated, more *dramatical* in spirit, if not in form, it will not have the qualities which can powerfully affect Englishmen. Not only were the Poets of our most national age dramatists, but there seems an evident dramatical tendency in those who wrote what we are wont to call narrative, or epic, poems. Take away the dramatic faculty from Chaucer, and the *Canterbury Tales* become indeed, what they have been most untruly called, mere versions of French or Italian Fables. Milton may have been right in changing the form of *Paradise Lost*, — we are bound to believe that he was right; for what appeal can there be against his genius? But he could not destroy the essentially dramatic character of a work which sets forth the battle between good and evil, and the Will of Man at once the Theatre and the Prize of the conflict. Is it not true, that there is in the very substance of the English mind, that which naturally predisposes us to sympathy with the Drama, and this though we are, perhaps, the most untheatrical of all people? The love of action, the impatience of abstraction, the equity which leads us to desire that every one may have a fair hearing, the reserve which had rather detect personal experience than have it announced — tendencies all easily perverted to evil, often leading to results the most contradictory, yet capable of the noblest cultivation, seem to explain the fact, that writers of this kind should have flourished so greatly among us, and that scarcely any others should permanently interest us.

These remarks do not concern poetical literature alone, or chiefly. Those habits of mind, of which I have spoken, ought to make us the best *historians*. If Germany has a right to claim the whole realm of the abstract, if Frenchmen understand the framework of society better than we do, there is in the national dramas of Shakspeare an historical secret which neither the philosophy of the one nor the acute observation of the other can discover. Yet these dramas are almost the only satisfactory expression of that historical faculty, which, I believe, is latent in us. The zeal of our factions, a result of our national activity, has made earnest history dishonest; our English justice has fled to indifferent and skeptical writers for the impartiality which it sought in vain elsewhere. This resource has failed, — the indifferentism of Hume could not secure him against his Scotch prejudices, or against gross unfairness when any thing disagreeably positive and vehement came in his way. Moreover, a practical people demand movement and life, not mere judging and balancing. For a time there was a reaction in favour of party history, but it could not last long; already we are glad to seek in Ranke or Michelet that which seems denied us at home. Much, no doubt, may be gained from such sources; but I am convinced that *this* is not the produce which we are meant generally to import; for this we may trust to well-directed native industry. The time is, I hope, at hand, when those who are most in earnest will feel that therefore they are most bound to be just — when they will confess the exceeding wickedness of the desire to extort or suppress a fact, or misrepresent a character — when they will ask as solemnly to be delivered from the temptation to this, as to any crime which is punished by law.

The clergy ought especially to lead the way in this reformation. They have erred grievously in perverting history to their own purposes. What was a sin in others was in them a blasphemy, because they professed to acknowledge God as the Ruler of the world, and hereby they showed that they valued their own conclusions above the facts which reveal His order. They owe, therefore, a great *amende* to their country, and they should consider seriously how they can make it most effectually. I look upon this Play as an effort in this direction, which I trust may be followed by many more. On this ground alone, even if its poetical worth was less than I believe it is, I should, as a clergyman, be thankful for its publication.

F. D. M.

INTRODUCTION

TO THE

SAINT'S TRAGEDY.

THE story which I have here put into a dramatic form is one familiar to Romanists, and perfectly and circumstantially authenticated. Abridged versions of it, carefully softened and sentimentalized, may be read in any Romish collection of Lives of the Saints. An enlarged edition has been published in France, I believe by Count Montalembert, and translated, with illustrations, by an English gentleman. From consulting this work I have hitherto abstained, in order that I might draw my facts and opinions, entire and unbiased, from the original Biography of Elizabeth, by Dietrich of Appold, her contemporary, as given entire by Canisius.

Dietrich was born in Thuringia, near the scene of Elizabeth's labours, a few years before her death, had conversed with those who had seen her, and calls to witness "God and the elect angels," that he had inserted nothing but what he had either understood from religious and veracious persons, or read in approved writings, viz: "*The Book of the Sayings of Elizabeth's Four Ladies* (*Guta, Isentrudis, and two others.*)" "*The Letter which Conrad of Marpurg, her Director, wrote to Pope Gregory the Ninth.*" (These two documents still exist.) "*The Sermon of Otto,*" (*de Ordine Prædic.*) "*which begins thus, Mulierem fortem.*"

"Not satisfied with these," he "visited monasteries, castles, and towns, interrogated the most aged and veracious persons, and wrote letters, seeking for completeness and truth in all things;" and thus composed his biography, from which that in Surius, (*Acta Sanctorum,*) Jacobus de Voragine, Alban Butler, and all others which I have seen, are copied with a very few additions and many prudent omissions.

Wishing to adhere strictly to historical truth, I have followed the received account, not only in the incidents, but often in the language which it attributes to its various characters; and have given in the Notes all necessary references to the biography in Canisius's collection. My part has therefore been merely to show how the conduct of my heroine was not only possible, but to a certain degree necessary, for a character of earnestness and piety such as hers, working under the influences of the Middle Age.

In deducing fairly, from the phenomena of her life, the character of Elizabeth, she necessarily became a type of two great mental struggles of the Middle Age; first, of that between Scriptural or unconscious, and

Popish or conscious, purity; in a word, between innocence and prudery; next, of the struggle between healthy human affection, and the Manichean contempt with which a celibate clergy would have all men regard the names of husband, wife, and parent. To exhibit this latter falsehood in its miserable consequences, when received into a heart of insight and determination sufficient to follow out all belief to its ultimate practice, is the main object of my Poem. That a most degrading and agonizing contradiction on these points must have existed in the mind of Elizabeth, and of all who with similar characters shall have found themselves under similar influences, is a necessity that must be evident to all who know any thing of the deeper affections of men. In the idea of a married Romish saint, these miseries should follow logically from the Romish view of human relations. In Elizabeth's case, their existence is proved equally logically from the acknowledged facts of her conduct.

I may here observe, that if I have in no case made her allude to the Virgin Mary, and exhibited the sense of infinite duty and loyalty to Christ alone, as the mainspring of all her noblest deeds, it is merely in accordance with Dietrich's biography. The omission of all Mariolatry is remarkable. My business is to copy that omission, as I should in the opposite case have copied the introduction of Virgin-worship into the original tale. The business of those who make Mary, to women especially, the complete substitute for the Saviour, — I had almost said, for all Three Persons of the Trinity, is to explain, if they can, her non-appearance in this case.

Lewis, again, I have drawn as I found him, possessed of all virtues but those of action; in knowledge, in moral courage, in spiritual attainment, infinitely inferior to his wife, and depending on her to be taught to pray; giving her higher faculties nothing to rest on in himself, and leaving the noblest offices of a husband to be supplied by a spiritual director. He thus becomes a type of the husbands of the Middle Age, and of the woman-worship of chivalry. Woman-worship, "the honour due to the weaker vessel," is indeed of God, and woe to the nation and to the man in whom it dies. But in the Middle Age, this feeling had no religious root, by which it could connect itself rationally, either with actual wedlock or with the noble yearnings of men's spirits, and it therefore could not but die down into a semi-sensual dream of female-saint-worship, or fantastic idolatry of mere physical beauty, leaving the women themselves an easy prey to the intellectual allurements of the more educated and subtle priesthood.

In Conrad's case, again, I have fancied that I discover, in the various notices of his life, a noble nature warped and blinded by its unnatural exclusions from those family ties through which we first discern or describe God and our relations to Him, and forced to concentrate his whole faculties in the service, not so much of a God of Truth as of a Catholic system. In his character will be found, I hope, some implicit apology for the failings of such truly great men as Dunstan, Becket, and Dominic, and of many more whom, if we hate, we shall never understand, while we shall be but too likely, in our own way to copy them.

Walter of Varila, a more fictitious character, represents the "healthy animalism" of the Teutonic mind, with its mixture of deep earnestness and hearty merriment. His dislike of priestly sentimentalities is no anachronism. Even in his day, a noble lay-religion, founded on faith in the divine and universal symbolism of humanity and nature, was gradually arising, and venting itself, from time to time, as I conceive, through many most unsuspected channels, through chivalry, through the minne-singers, through the lay-inventors, or rather importers, of pointed architecture, through the German school of painting, through the politics of the free-towns, till it attained complete freedom, in Luther and his associate reformers.

For my fantastic quotations of Scripture, if they shall be deemed irreverent, I can only say, that they were the fashion of the time, from prince to peasant — that there is scarcely one of them, with which I have not actually met in the writings of the period — that those writings abound with misuse of Scripture, far more coarse, arbitrary, and ridiculous, than any which I have dared to insert — that I had no right to omit so radical a characteristic of the Middle Age.

For the more coarse and homely passages with which the drama is interspersed, I must make the same apology.

I put them there because they were there — because the Middle Age was, in the gross, a coarse, barbarous, and profligate age — because it was necessary, in order to bring out fairly, the beauty of the central character, to show "the crooked and perverse generation," in which she was "a child of God without rebuke." It was, in fact, the very ferocity and foulness of the time which, by a natural revulsion, called forth at the same time, the apostolic holiness, and the Manichean asceticism of the Medieval Saints. The world was so bad, that to be Saints at all, they were compelled to go out of the world. It was necessary, moreover, in depicting the poor man's patroness, to show the material on which she worked; and those who know the poor, know also that we can no more judge truly of their characters in the presence of their benefactors, than we can tell by seeing clay in the potter's hands, what it was in its native pit. These scenes have, therefore, been laid principally in Elizabeth's absence, in order to preserve their only use and meaning.

So rough and common life a picture of the Middle Age will, I am afraid, whether faithful or not, be far from acceptable, to those who take their notions of that period principally from such exquisite dreams as the fictions of Fouqué, and of certain moderns whose graceful minds, like some enchanted well,

> In whose calm depths the pure and beautiful
> Alone are mirrored,

are, on account of their very sweetness and simplicity,

singularly unfitted to convey any true likeness of the coarse and stormy Middle Age. I have been already accused, by others than Romanists, of profaning this whole subject — i. e. of telling the whole truth, pleasant or not, about it. But really, time enough has been lost in ignorant abuse of that period, and time enough, also, lately, in blind adoration of it. When shall we learn to see it as it was? — the dawning manhood of Europe — rich with all the tenderness, the simplicity, the enthusiasm of youth — but also darkened, alas! with its full share of youth's precipitance and extravagance, fierce passions, and blind self-will — its virtues and its vices colossal, and, for that very reason, always haunted by the twin-imp of the colossal — the caricatured.

Lastly, the many miraculous stories which the biographer of Elizabeth relates of her, I had no right, for the sake of truth, to interweave in the plot, while it was necessary to indicate, at least, their existence. I have, therefore, put such of them as seemed least absurd into the mouth of Conrad, to whom, in fact, they owe their original publication, and have done so, as I hope, not without a just ethical purpose.

Such was my idea; of the inconsistencies and shortcomings of this its realization, no one can ever be so painfully sensible, as I am already myself. If, however, this book shall cause one Englishman honestly to ask himself, "I, as a Protestant, have been accustomed to assert the purity and dignity of the offices of husband, wife, and parent. Have I ever examined the grounds of my own assertion? Do I believe them to be, as callings from God, spiritual, sacramental, divine, eternal? Or am I at heart regarding and using them, like the Papist, merely as heaven's indulgences to the infirmities of fallen man?" — Then will my book have done its work.

If, again, it shall deter one young man from the example of those miserable dilettanti, who in books and sermons are whimpering meagre second-hand praises of celibacy, — depreciating as carnal and degrading those family ties, to which they owe their own existence, in the enjoyment of which they themselves all the while unblushingly indulge — insulting thus their own wives and mothers, — nibbling ignorantly at the very root of that household purity, which constitutes the distinctive superiority of Protestant over Popish nations; — again my book will have done its work.

If, lastly, it shall awake one pious Protestant to recognize, in some, at least, of the Saints of the Middle Age, beings not only of the same passions, but of the same Lord, the same faith, the same baptism, as themselves; *Protestants*, not the less deep and true, because utterly unconscious and practical — mighty witnesses against the two antichrists of their age — the tyranny of feudal caste, and the phantoms which Popery substitutes for the living Christ — then also will my little book indeed have done its work.

C. K.

THE SAINT'S TRAGEDY.

CHARACTERS.

ELIZABETH, *daughter of the King of Hungary.*

LEWIS, *Landgrave of Thuringia, betrothed to her in childhood.*

HENRY, *brother of Lewis.*

WALTER, *of Varila,*
RUDOLF, *the Cupbearer,*
LEUTOLF, *of Erlstetten,*
HARTWIG, *of Erba,*
COUNT HUGO,
COUNT OF SAYM, &c. } *Vassals of Lewis.*

CONRAD, *of Marpurg, a Monk, the Pope's Commissioner for the suppression of heresy.*

GERARD, *his Chaplain.*

BISHOP OF BAMBERG, *uncle of Elizabeth, &c. &c.*

SOPHIA, *Dowager Landgravine.*

AGNES, *her daughter, sister of Lewis.*

ISENTRUDIS, *Elizabeth's nurse.*

GUTA, *her favourite maiden.*

&c. &c. &c.

The Scene lies principally in Eisenach, and the Wartburg; changing afterwards to Bamberg, and finally to Marpurg.

PROEM.

(EPIMETHEUS.)

I.

WAKE again, Teutonic Father-ages,
  Speak again, beloved primæval creeds;
Flash ancestral spirit from your pages,
  Wake the greedy age to noble deeds.

II.

Tell us, how of old our saintly mothers
  Schooled themselves by vigil, fast, and prayer;
Learnt to love as Jesus loved before them,
  While they bore the cross which poor men bear.

III.

Tell us how our stout crusading fathers
  Fought and died for God, and not for gold;
Let their love, their faith, their boyish daring,
  Distance-mellowed, gild the days of old.

IV.

Tell us how the sexless workers, thronging,
  Angel-tended, round the convent doors,
Wrought to Christian faith and holy order
  Savage hearts alike and barren moors.

V.

Ye who built the churches where we worship,
  Ye who framed the laws by which we move,
Fathers, long belied, and long forsaken,
  Oh! forgive the children of your love!

(PROMETHEUS.)

I.

Speak! but ask us not to be as ye were!
  All but God is changing day by day.
He who breathes on man the plastic spirit,
  Bids us mould ourselves its robe of clay.

II.

Old anarchic floods of revolution,
  Drowning ill and good alike in night,
Sink, and bear the wrecks of ancient labour,
  Fossil-teeming, to the searching light!

III.

There will we find laws, which shall interpret,
  Through the simpler past, existing life;
Delving up from mines and fairy caverns
  Charmed blades, to cut the age's strife.

IV.

What though fogs may stream from draining waters?
  We will till the clays to mellow loam;
Wake the graveyard of our fathers' spirits;
  Clothe its crumbling mounds with blade and bloom.

V.

Old decays but foster new creations;
  Bones and ashes feed the golden corn;
Fresh elixirs wander every moment,
  Down the veins through which the live past feeds
    its child, the live unborn.

THE SAINT'S TRAGEDY.

ACT I.

Scene I. A.D. 1220.

The Doorway of a closed Chapel in the Wartburg. Elizabeth *sitting on the Steps.*

Eliz. Baby Jesus, who dost lie
Far above that stormy sky,
In Thy mother's pure caress,
Stoop and save the motherless.

Happy birds! whom Jesus leaves
Underneath his sheltering eaves;
There they go to play and sleep,
May not I go in to weep?

All without is mean and small,
All within is vast and tall;
All without is harsh and shrill,
All within is hushed and still.

Jesus, let me enter in,
Wrap me safe from noise and sin;
Let me list the angels' songs,
See the picture of Thy wrongs;

Let me kiss Thy wounded feet,
Drink Thine incense, faint and sweet,
While the clear bells call Thee down
From Thine everlasting throne.

At Thy door-step low I bend,
Who have neither kin nor friend;
Let me here a shelter find,
Shield the shorn lamb from the wind.

Jesu, Lord, my heart will break,
Save me for Thy great love's sake!

Enter ISENTRUDIS.

Isen. Aha! I had missed my little bird from the nest,
And judged that she was here. What 's this? fie, tears?
Eliz. Go! you despise me like the rest.
Isen. Despise you?
What 's here? King Andrew's child? St. John's sworn maid?
Who dares despise you? Out upon these Saxons!
They sang another note when I was younger,
When from the rich East came my queenly pearl,
Lapt on this fluttering heart, while mighty heroes

Rode by her side, and far behind us stretched
The barbs and sumpter mules, a royal train,
Laden with silks and furs, and priceless gems,
Wedges of gold, and furniture of silver,
Fit for my princess.

Eliz. Hush now, I've heard all, nurse,
A thousand times.

Isen. Oh, how their hungry mouths
Did water at the booty! Such a prize,
Since the three Kings came wandering into Cöln,
They ne'er saw, nor their fathers;—well they knew it!
Oh, how they fawned on us! "Great Isentrudis!"
"Sweet babe!" The Landgravine did thank her saints
As if you, or your silks, had fallen from heaven;
And now she wears your furs, and calls us gipsies.
Come tell your nurse your griefs; we 'll weep together,
Strangers in this strange land!

Eliz. I am most friendless.
The Landgravine and Agnes—you may see them
Begrudge the food I eat, and call me friend
Of knaves and serving-maids; the burly knights
Freeze me with cold blue eyes: no saucy page
But points and whispers, "There goes our pet nun;
Would but her saintship leave her gold behind,
We 'd give herself her furlough." Save me! save me!
All here are ghastly dreams; dead masks of stone,
And you and I, and Guta, only live:
Your eyes alone have souls. I shall go mad!
Oh! that they would but leave me all alone,

To teach poor girls and work within my chamber,
With mine own thoughts, and all the gentle angels
Which glance about my dreams at morning-tide;
Then I should be as happy as the birds
Which sing at my bower window. Once I longed
To be beloved,—now would they but forget me!
Most vile I must be, or they could not hate me!

Isen. They are of this world, thou art not, poor child,
Therefore they hate thee, as they did thy betters.

Eliz. But, Lewis, nurse?

Isen. He, child? he is thy knight;
Espoused from childhood: thou hast a claim upon him.
One that thou 'lt need, alas!—though, I remember—
'Tis fifteen years agone—when in one cradle
We laid two fair babes for a marriage token;
And when your lips met, then you smiled, and twined
Your little limbs together.—Pray the Saints
That token stand!—He calls thee love and sister,
And brings thee gewgaws from the wars; that 's much!
At least he 's thine if thou love him.

Eliz. If I love him?
What is this love? Why, is he not my brother
And I his sister? Till these weary wars,
The one of us without the other never
Did weep or laugh: what is 't should change us now?
You shake your head and smile.

Isen. Go to; the chafe
Comes not by wearing chains but feeling them.

Eliz. Alas! here comes a knight across the court;
O, hide me, nurse! What 's here? this door is fast.

Isen. Nay, 'tis a friend: he brought my princess hither,
Walter of Varila; I feared him once—
He used to mock our state, and say, good wine
Should want no bush, and that the cage was gay,
But that the bird must sing before he praised it.
Yet he 's a kind heart, while his bitter tongue
Awes these court popinjays at times to manners.
He will smile sadly too, when he meets my maiden;
And once he said, he was your liegeman sworn,
Since my lost mistress weeping, to his charge
Trusted the babe she saw no more.—God help us!

Eliz. How did my mother die, nurse?

Isen. She died, my child.

Eliz. But how? Why turn away?
Too long I've guessed at some dread mystery
I may not hear: and in my restless dreams,
Night after night, sweeps by a frantic rout
Of grinning fiends, fierce horses, bodiless hands,
Which clutch at one to whom my spirit yearns
As to a mother. There 's some fearful tie
Between me and that spirit-world, which God
Brands with His terrors on my troubled mind.
Speak! tell me, nurse! is she in heaven or hell?

Isen. God knows, my child: there are masses for her soul,
Each day in every Zingar minster sung.

Eliz. But was she holy?—Died she in the Lord?

Isen. (*weeps.*) Oh, God! my child! And if I told thee all,
How could'st thou mend it?

Eliz. Mend it? Oh, my Saviour!
I'd die a saint!
Win heaven for her by prayers, and build great minsters,
Chantries, and hospitals for her; wipe out
By mighty deeds our race's guilt and shame—
But thus, poor witless orphan! (*Weeps.*)

COUNT WALTER *enters.*

Wal. Ah! my princess! accept your liegeman's knee;
Down, down, rheumatic flesh!

Eliz. Ah! Count Walter! you are too tall to kneel to little girls.

Wal. What? shall two hundred weight of hypocrisy bow down to his four-inch wooden saint, and the same weight of honesty not worship his four-foot live one? And I have a jest for you, shall make my small queen merry and wise.

Isen. You shall jest long before she 's merry.

Wal. Ah! dowers and dowagers again! The money—root of all evil.
What comes here? [*A Page enters.*
A long-winged grasshopper, all gold, green, and gauze! How these young pea-chicks must needs ape the grown peacock's frippery! Prithee, now, how many such butterflies as you suck here together on the thistle-head of royalty?

Page. Some twelve gentlemen of us, Sir—apostles of the blind archer, Love—owning no divinity but almighty beauty—no faith, no hope, no charity, but those which are kindled at her eyes.

Wal. Saints! what 's all this?

Page. Ah, Sir! none but countrymen swear by the saints nowadays: no oaths but allegorical ones, Sir, at the high table; as thus,—"By the sleeve of beauty, Madam;" or again, "By Love his martyrdoms, Sir Count," or to a potentate, "As Jove's imperial mercy shall hear my vows, High Mightiness."

Wal. Where did the evil one set you on finding all this heathenry?

Page. Oh! we are all barristers of Love's court, Sir, —we have Ovid's gay science conned, Sir, *ad unguentum*, as they say, out of the French book.

Wal. So? There are those come from Rome then will whip you and Ovid out with the same rod which the dandies of Provence felt lately to their sorrow. Oh! what blinkards are we gentlemen, to train any dumb beasts more carefully than we do Christians;—that a man shall keep his dog-breakers, and his horse-breakers, and his hawk-breakers, and never hire him a boy-breaker or two! that we should live without a qualm at dangling such a flock of mimicking parroquets at our heels awhile, and then when they are well infected, well perfumed with the wind of our vices, dropping them off, as tadpoles do their tails, joint by joint, into the mud! to strain at such gnats as an ill-mouthed colt or a riotous puppy, and swallow that camel of camels, a page!

Page. Do you call me a camel, Sir?

Wal. What's your business?

Page. My errand is to the princess here.

Eliz. To me?

Page. Yes; the Landgravine expects you at high mass; so go in, and mind you clean yourself; for every one is not as fond as you of beggars' brats, and what their clothes leave behind them.

Isen. (*Strikes him.*) Monkey! To whom are you speaking?

Eliz. Oh, peace, peace, peace! I'll go with him.

Page. Then be quick, my music-master's waiting. Corpo di Bacco! as if our elders did not teach us to whom we ought to be rude! [*Ex.* ELIZ. *and Page.*

Isen. See here, Sir Saxon, how this pearl of price
Is faring in your hands! The peerless image,
To whom this court is but the tawdry frame,—
The speck of light amid its murky baseness,—
The salt which keeps it all from rotting,—cast
To be the common fool,—the laughing-stock
For every beardless knave to whet his wit on!
Tar-blooded Germans!—Here's another of them.

[*A young Knight enters.*

Knight. Heigh! Count! What? learning to sing psalms? They are waiting
For you in the manage-school, to give your judgment
On that new Norman mare.

Wal. Tell them I'm busy.

Knight. Busy? St. Martin! Knitting stockings, eh?
To clothe the poor withal? Is that your business?

I passed that canting baby on the stairs;
Would Heaven that she had tripped and broke her goose-
neck,
And left us heirs de facto. So, farewell. [*Exit.*

Wal. A very pretty quarrel! matter enough
To spoil a wagon-load of ash-staves on,
And break a dozen fools' backs across their cantlets.
What's Lewis doing?

Isen. Oh—Befooled,—
Bewitched with dogs and horses, like an idiot
Clutching his bauble, while a priceless jewel
Sticks at his miry heels.

Wal. The boy's no fool,—
As good a heart as her's, but somewhat given
To hunt the nearest butterfly, and light
The fire of fancy without hanging o'er it
The porridge-pot of practice. He shall hear on't.

Isen. And quickly, for there's treason in the wind.
They'll keep her dower, and send her home with shame
Before the year's out.

Wal. Humph! Some are rogues enough for't. As it falls out, I ride with him to-day.

Isen. Upon what business?

Wal. Some shaveling has been telling him that there are heretics on his land; stadings, worshippers of black cats, baby-eaters, and such like. He consulted me; I told him it would be time enough to see to the heretics, when all the good Christians had been well looked after. I suppose the novelty of the thing smit him, for now nothing will serve but I must ride with him round half a dozen hamlets, where, with God's help, I will show him a manstye or two, that shall astonish his delicate chivalry.

Isen. O, here 's your time! Speak to him, noble Walter.
Stun his dull ears with praises of her grace;
Prick his dull heart with shame at his own coldness.
O, right us, Count.

Wal. I will, I will: go in
And dry your eyes. [*Exeunt separately.*

SCENE II.

A Landscape in Thuringia. LEWIS *and* WALTER *riding.*

Lew. So all these lands are mine; these yellow meads—
These village-greens, and forest-fretted hills,
With dizzy castles crowned. Mine? Why that word
Is rich in promise, in the action bankrupt.
What faculty of mine, save dream-fed pride
Can these things fatten? Mass! I had forgot:
I have a right to bark at trespassers.
Rare privilege! While every fowl and bush,
According to its destiny and nature,
(Which were they truly mine, my power could alter)
Will live, and grow, and take no thought of me.
Those firs, before whose stealthy-marching ranks
The world-old oaks still dwindle and retreat,
If I could stay their poisoned frown, which cows
The pale, shrunk underwood, and nestled seeds

Into an age of sleep, 'twere something; and those men
O'er whom that one word "ownership" uprears me—
If I could make them lift a finger up
But of their own free will, I'd own my seisin.
But now—when if I sold them, life and limb,
There 's not a sow would litter one pig less
Than when men called her mine.—Possession's naught—
A parchment ghost; a word I am ashamed
To claim even here, lest all the forest spirits,
And bees who drain unasked the free-born flowers,
Should mock, and cry, "Vain man, not thine, but ours."

Wal. Possession 's naught? Possession 's beef and ale—
Soft bed, fair wife, gay horse, good steel.—Are they naught?
Possession means to sit astride of the world,
Instead of having it astride of you;
Is that naught? 'Tis the easiest trade of all too;
For he that 's fit for nothing else, is fit
To own good land, and on the slowest dolt
His state sits easiest, while his serfs thrive best.

Lew. How now? What need then of long discipline
Not to mere feats of arms, but feats of soul;
To courtesies and high self-sacrifice,
To order and obedience, and the grace
Which makes commands requests,—and service favour?
To faith and prayer, and pure thoughts, ever turned
To that Valhalla, where the virgin saints
And stainless heroes tend the Queen of heaven?

Why these, if I but need, like stalled ox,
To chew the grass cut for me?
Wal. Why? Because
I have trained thee for a knight, boy, not a ruler.
All callings want their proper 'prentice time
But this of ruling; it comes by mother-wit;
And if the wit be not exceeding great,
'Tis best the wit be most exceeding small;
And he that holds the reins, should let the horse
Range on, feed where he will, live and let live.
Custom and selfishness will keep all steady
For half a life.—Six months before you die
You may begin to think of interfering.
Lew. Alas! while each day blackens with fresh clouds,
Complaints of ague, fever, crumbling huts,
Of land thrown out to the forest, game and keepers,
Bailiffs and barons, plundering all alike;
Need, greed, stupidity: To clear such ruin
Would task the rich prime of some noble hero—
But can I nothing do?
Wal. Oh! plenty, Sir;
Which no man yet has done or e'er will do.
It rests with you, whether the priest be honoured;
It rests with you, whether the knight be knightly;
It rests with you, whether those fields grow corn;
It rests with you, whether those toiling peasants
Lift to their masters free and loyal eyes,
Or crawl, like jaded hacks, to welcome graves.
It rests with you—and will rest.

Lew. I'll crowd my court and dais with men of God,
As doth my peerless namesake, King of France.
Wal. Priests, Sir? The Frenchman keeps two counsellors
Worth any drove of priests.
Lew. And who are they?
Wal. God and his lady-love. (*Aside.*) He 'll open at that—
Lew. I could be that man's squire.
Wal. (*Aside.*) Again run riot—
Now for another cast; (*Aloud.*) If you 'd sleep sound, Sir,
You 'll let priests pray for you, but school you never.
Lew. Mass! who more fitted?
Wal. None, if you could trust them;
But they are the people's creatures; poor men give them
Their power at the Church, and take it back at the alehouse:
Then what 's the friar to the starving peasant?
Just what the abbot is to the greedy noble—
A scarecrow to lear wolves. Go ask the churchplate,
Safe in knight's cellars, how these priests are feared.
Bruised reeds when you most need them.—No, my Lord;
Copy them, trust them never.
Lew. Copy? wherein?
Wal. In letting every man
Do what he likes, and only seeing he does it
As you do your work—well. That 's the Church secret
For breeding towns, as fast as you breed roe-deer;

Example, but no meddling. See that hollow—
I knew it once all heath, and deep peat-bog—
I drowned a black mare in that self-same spot
Hunting with your good father: Well, he gave it,
One jovial night, to six poor Erfurt monks—
Six picked-visaged, wan, bird-fingered wights—
All in their rough hair shirts, like hedgehogs starved—
I told them, six weeks' work would break their hearts;
They answered, Christ would help, and Christ's great mother,
And make them strong when weakest: So they settled:
And starved and froze.

Lew. And dug and built, it seems.

Wal. Faith, that 's true. See—as garden walls draw snails,
They have drawn a hamlet round; the slopes are blue
Knee-deep with flax, the orchard boughs are breaking
With strange outlandish fruits. See those young rogues
Marching to school; no poachers here, Lord Landgrave,—
Too much to be done at home; there 's not a village
Of yours, now, thrives like this: By God's good help
These men have made their ownership worth something.
Here comes one of them.

Lew. I would speak to him—
And learn his secret—We 'll await him here.

Enter CONRAD.

Con. Peace to you, reverend and war-worn knight,
And you, fair youth, upon whose swarthy lip

Blooms the rich promise of a noble manhood.
Methinks, if simple monks may read your thoughts,
That with no envious or distasteful eyes
Ye watch the labours of God's poor elect.

Wal. Why—we were saying, how you cunning rooks
Pitch as by instinct on the fattest fallows.

Con. For He who feeds the ravens, promiseth
Our bread and water sure, and leads us on
By peaceful streams in pastures green to lie,
Beneath our Shepherd's eye.

Lew. In such a nook, now,
To nestle from this noisy world—

Con. —And drop
The burden of thyself upon the threshold.

Lew. Think what rich dreams may haunt those lowly roofs!

Con. Rich dreams,—and more; their dreams will find fulfilment—
Their discipline breeds strength—'Tis we alone
Can join the patience of the laboring ox
Unto the eagle's foresight,—not a fancy
Of ours, but grows in time to mighty deeds;
Victories in heavenly warfare: but yours, yours, Sir,
Oh choke them, choke the panting hopes of youth,
Ere they be born, and wither in slow pains,
Cast by for the next bauble!

Lew. 'Tis too true!
I dread no toil: toil is the true knight's pastime—
Faith fails, the will intense and fixed, so easy

To thee, cut off from life and love, whose powers
In one close channel must condense their stream:
But I, to whom this life blooms rich and busy,
Whose heart goes out a-Maying all the year
In this new Eden—in my fitful thought
What skill is there, to turn my faith to sight—
To pierce blank Heaven, like some trained falconer
After his game, beyond all human ken?

Wal. And walk into the bog beneath your feet.

Con. And change it to firm land by magic step!
Build there cloud-cleaving spires, beneath whose shade
Great cities rise for vassals; to call forth
From plough and loom the rank unlettered hinds,
And make them saints and heroes—send them forth
To sway with heavenly craft the spirit of princes;
Change nations' destinies, and conquer worlds
With love, more mighty than the sword; what, Count?
Art thou ambitious? practical? we monks
Can teach you somewhat there too.

Lew. Be it so;
But love you have foresworn; and what were life
Without that chivalry, which bends man's knees
Before God's image and his glory, best
Revealed in woman's beauty?

Con. Ah! poor worldlings!
Little you dream what maddening ecstasies,
What rich ideals haunt, by day and night,
Alone, and in the crowd, even to the death,
The servitors of that celestial court

Where peerless Mary, sun-enthroned, reigns,
In whom all Eden dreams of womanhood,
All grace of form, hue, sound, all beauty strewn
Like pearls unstrung, about this ruined world,
Have their fulfilment and their archetype.
Why hath the rose its scent, the lily grace?
To mirror forth her loveliness, from whom,
Primeval fount of grace, their livery came:
Pattern of Seraphs! only worthy ark
To bear her God athwart the floods of time!

Lew. Who dare aspire to her? Alas, not I!
To me she is a doctrine, and a picture:—
I cannot live on dreams.

Con. She hath her train:—
There thou may'st choose thy love: If world-wide lore
Shall please thee, and the Cherub's glance of fire,
Let Catharine lift thy soul, and rapt with her
Question the mighty dead, until thou float
Tranced on the ethereal ocean of her spirit.
If pity father passion in thee, hang
Above Eulalia's tortured loveliness;
And for her sake, and in her strength, go forth
To do and suffer greatly. Dost thou long
For some rich heart, as deep in love as weakness,
Whose wild simplicity sweet heaven-born instincts
Alone keep sane?

Lew. I do, I do. I'd live
And die for each and all the three.

Con. Then go—
Entangled in the Magdalen's tresses lie;
Dream hours before her picture, till thy lips
Dare to approach her feet, and thou shalt start
To find the canvas warm with life, and matter
A moment transubstantiate to heaven.

Wal. Ay, catch his fever, Sir, and learn to take
An indigestion for a troop of angels.
Come tell him, monk, about your magic gardens,
Where not a stringy head of kale is cut
But breeds a vision or a revelation.

Lew. Hush, hush, Count! Speak, strange monk, strange words, and waken
Longings more strange than either.

Con. Then, if proved,
As I dare vouch thee, loyal in thy love,
Even to the Queen herself thy saintlier soul
At length may soar: perchance—Oh, bliss too great
For thought—yet possible!
Receive some token—smile—or hallowing touch
Of that white hand, beneath whose soft caress
The raging world is smoothed, and runs its course
To shadow forth her glory.

Lew. Thou dost tempt me—
That were a knightly quest.

Con. Ay, here 's true love.
Love's heaven, without its hell; the golden fruit
Without the foul husk, which at Adam's fall
Did crust it o'er with filth and selfishness.

I tempt thee heavenward—from yon azure walls
Unearthly beauties beckon—God's own mother
Waits longing for thy choice—

Lew. Is this a dream?

Wal. Ay, by the Living Lord, who died for you!
Will you be cozened, Sir, by these air-blown fancies,
These male hysterics, by starvation bred
And huge conceit? Cast off God's gift of manhood,
And like the dog in the adage, drop the true bone
With snapping at the sham one in the water?
What were you born a man for?

Lew. Ay, I know it:—
I cannot live on dreams. Oh, for one friend,
Myself, yet not myself; one not so high
But she could love me, not too pure to pardon
My sloth and meanness! Oh! for flesh and blood,
Before whose feet I could adore, yet love!
How easy then were duty! From her lips
To learn my daily task;—in her pure eyes
To see the living type of those heaven-glories
I dare not look on;—let her work her will
Of love and wisdom on these straining hinds;—
To squire a saint around her labour field,
And she and it both mine:—That were possession!

Con. The flesh, fair youth—

Wal. Avaunt, bald snake, avaunt!
We are past your burrow now. Come, come, Lord
Landgrave,
Look round, and find your saint.

Lew. Alas! one such—
One such, I know, who upward from one cradle
Beside me like a sister—No, thank God! no sister!—
Has grown and grown, and with her mellow shade
Has blanched my thornless thoughts to her own hue,
And even now is budding into blossom,
Which never shall bear fruit, but inward still
Resorb its vital nectar, self-contained,
And leave no living copies of its beauty
To after ages. Ah! be less, sweet maid,
Less than thyself! Yet no—my wife thou might'st be,
If less than thus—but not the saint thou art.
What! shall my selfish longings drag thee down
From maid to wife? degrade the soul I worship?
That were a caitiff deed! Oh, misery!
Is wedlock treason to that purity,
Which is the jewel and the soul of wedlock?
Elizabeth! my saint! [*Exit* CONRAD.

Wal. What, Sir? the Princess?
Ye saints in heaven, I thank you!

Lew. Oh, who else,
Who else the minutest lineament fulfils
Of this my cherished portrait?

Wal. So—'tis well.
Hear me, my Lord.—You think this dainty princess
Too perfect for you, eh? That 's well again:
For that whose price after fruition falls
May well too high be rated ere enjoyed—
In plain words,—if she looks an angel now, you will be

better mated than you expected, when you find her—a woman. For flesh and blood she is, and that young blood,—whom her childish misusage and your brotherly love; her loneliness and your protection; her springing fancy and (for I may speak to you as a son) your beauty and knightly grace have so bewitched, and, as some say, degraded, that briefly, she loves you, and briefly, better, her few friends fear, than you love her.

Lew. Loves me! My Count, that word is quickly spoken;
And yet, if it be true, it thrusts me forth
Upon a shoreless sea of untried passion,
From whence is no return.

Wal. By Siegfried's sword,
My words are true, and I came here to say them,
To thee, my son in all but blood.
Mass, I'm no gossip. Why? What ails the boy?

Lew. Loves me! Henceforth, let no man, peering down
Through the dim glittering mine of future years,
Say to himself "Too much! this cannot be!"
To-day, and custom, wall up our horizon:
Before the hourly miracle of life
Blindfold we stand, and sigh, as though God were not.
I have wandered in the mountains, mist-bewildered,
And now a breeze comes, and the veil is lifted,
And priceless flowers, o'er which I trod unheeding,
Gleam ready for my grasp. She loves me then!
She, who to me was as a nightingale

That sings in magic gardens, rock-beleaguered,
To passing angels melancholy music—
Whose dark eyes hung, like far-off evening stars,
Those rosy-cushioned windows coldly shining
Down from the cloud world of her unknown fancy—
She, for whom holiest touch of holiest knight
Seemed all too gross—who might have been a saint
And companied with angels—thus to pluck
The spotless rose of her own maidenhood
To give it unto me!

Wal. You love her then?

Lew. Look! If yon solid mountain were all gold,
And each particular tree a band of jewels,
And from its womb the Niebelungen hoard
With elfin wardens called me, "Leave thy love
And be our Master"—I would turn away—
And know no wealth but her.

Wal. Shall I say this to her?
I am no carrier pigeon, Sir, by breed,
But now, between her friends and persecutors
My life 's a burden.

Lew. Persecutors? Who?
Alas! I guess it—I had known my mother
Too light for that fair saint,—but who else dare wink
When she is by? My knights?

Wal. To a man, my Lord.

Lew. Here 's chivalry! Well, that 's soon brought to bar.
The quarrel 's mine; my lance shall clear that stain.

Wal. Quarrel with your knights? Cut your own chair-legs off!
They do but sail with the stream. Her passion, Sir,
Broke shell and ran out twittering before yours did,
And unrequited love is mortal sin
With this chaste world. My boy, my boy, I tell you,
The fault lies nearer home.

Lew. I have played the coward—
And in the sloth of false humility,
Cast by the pearl I dared not to deserve.
How laggard I must seem to her, though she love me;
Playing with hawks and hounds, while she sits weeping!
'Tis not too late.

Wal. Too late, my royal eyas?
You shall strike this deer yourself at gaze ere long—
She has no mind to slip to cover.

Lew. Come—
We'll back—we'll back; and you shall bear the message;
I am ashamed to speak. Tell her I love her—
That I should need to tell her! Say, my coyness
Was bred of worship, not of coldness.

Wal. Then the serfs
Must wait?

Lew. Why not? This day to them, too, blessing brings,
Which clears from envious webs their guardian angel's wings. [*Exeunt.*

SCENE III.

A Chamber in the Castle. SOPHIA, ELIZABETH, AGNES, ISENTRUDE, *&c., re-entering.*

Soph. What! you will not? You hear, dame Isentrude,
She will not wear her coronet in the church,
Because, forsooth, the crucifix within
Is crowned with thorns. You hear her.
Eliz. Noble mother,
How could I flaunt this bauble in His face
Who hung there, naked, bleeding, all for me—
I felt it shamelessness to go so gay.
Soph. Felt? What then? Every foolish wench has feelings
In these religious days, and thinks it carnal
To wash her dishes, and obey her parents—
No wonder they ape you, if you ape them—
Go to! I hate this humble-minded pride,
Self-willed submission—to your own pert fancies;
This fog-bed mushroom-spawn of brain-sick wits,
Who make their oddities their test for grace,
And peer about to catch the general eye;
Ah! I have watched you throw your playmates down
To have the pleasure of kneeling for their pardon.
Here 's sanctity—to shame your cousin and me—
Spurn rank and proper pride, and decency;—
If God has made you noble, use your rank,
If you but know how. You Landgravine? You mated

With gentle Lewis? Why, belike you'll cowl him,
As that stern prude, your aunt, cowled her poor spouse;
No—one Hedwiga at a time's enough,—
My son shall die no monk.

Isen. Beseech you, Madam,—
Weep not, my darling.

Soph. Tut—I'll speak my mind.
We'll have no saints. Thank heaven, my saintliness
Ne'er troubled my good man, by day or night.
We'll have no saints, I say; far better for you,
And no doubt pleasanter—You know your place—
At least you know your place,—to take to cloisters,
And there sit carding wool, and mumbling Latin,
With sour old maids, and maundering Magdalens,
Proud of your frost-kibed feet, and dirty serge.
There's nothing noble in you, but your blood;
And that one almost doubts. Who art thou, child?

Isen. The daughter, please your highness,
Of Andreas, king of Hungary, your better,
And your son's spouse.

Soph. I had forgotten, truly—
And you, Dame Isentrudis, are her servant,
And mine: come, Agnes, leave the gipsy ladies
To say their prayers, and set the Saints the fashion.

[SOPHIA *and* AGNES *go out*

Isen. Proud hussy! Thou shalt set thy foot on her neck yet, darling,
When thou art Landgravine.

Eliz. And when will that be?

No, she speaks truth! I should have been a nun.
These are the wages of my cowardice,—
Too weak to face the world, too weak to leave it!

Guta. I'll take the veil with you.

Eliz. 'Twere but a moment's work,—
To slip into the convent there below,
And be at peace forever. And you, my nurse?

Isen. I will go with thee, child, where'er thou goest.
But Lewis?

Eliz. Ah! my brother! No, I dare not—
I dare not turn forever from this hope,
Though it be dwindled to a thread of mist.
Oh! that we two could flee and leave this Babel!
Oh! if he were but some poor chapel-priest,
In lonely mountain valleys far away;
And I his serving-maid, to work his vestments,
And dress his scrap of food, and see him stand
Before the altar like a rainbowed saint,
To take the blessed wafer from his hand,
Confess my heart to him, and all night long
Pray for him while he slept, or through the lattice
Watch while he read, and see the holy thoughts
Swell in his big deep eyes.—Alas! that dream
Is wilder than the one that 's fading even now!
Who 's here? [*A Page enters.*

Page. The Count of Varila, madam, begs permission to speak with you.

Eliz. With me? What 's this new terror?
Tell him I wait him.

Isen. (*Aside.*) Ah! my old heart sinks—
God send us rescue! Here the champion comes.

COUNT WALTER *enters.*

Wal. Most learned, fair, and sanctimonious princess—
Plague, what comes next! I had something orthodox ready;
'Tis dropped out by the way.—Mass! here's the pith on't.—
Madam, I come a wooing; and for one
Who is as only worthy of your love,
As you of his; he bids me claim the spousals
Made long ago between you,—and yet leaves
Your fancy free, to grant, or pass that claim;
And being that Mercury is not my planet,
He hath advised himself to set herein,
With pen and ink, what seemed good to him,
As passport to this jewelled mirror, pledge
Unworthy of his worship. [*Gives a letter and jewel.*

Isen. Nunc Domine dimittis servam tuam!

[ELIZABETH *looks over the letter and casket, claps her hands, and bursts into childish laughter.*]

Why here's my Christmas tree come after Lent—
Espousals? pledges? by our childish love?
Pretty words for folks to think of at the wars,—
And pretty presents come of them! Look, Guta!
A crystal clear, and carven on the reverse,
The blessed rood. He told me once—one night,
When we did sit in the garden—What was I saying?

Wal. My fairest princess, as ambassador,
What shall I answer?

Eliz. Tell him—tell him—God!
Have I grown mad, or a child within the moment?
The earth has lost her gray sad hue, and blazes
With her old life-light; hark! yon wind 's a song—
Those clouds are angels' robes.—That fiery west
Is paved with smiling faces.—I am a woman,
And all things bid me love! my dignity
Is thus to cast my virgin pride away,
And find my strength in weakness.—Busy brain!
Thou keep'st pace with my heart; old lore, old fancies,
Buried for years, leap from their tombs, and proffer
Their magic service to my new-born spirit.
I'll go—I am not mistress of myself—
Send for him—bring him to me—he is mine! [*Exit.*

Isen. Ah! blessed Saints! how changed upon the moment!
She is grown taller, trust me, and her eye
Flames like a fresh caught hind's. She that was christened
A brown mouse for her stillness! Good my Lord!
Now shall mine old bones see the grave in peace!

SCENE IV.

The Bridal Feast. ELIZABETH, LEWIS, SOPHIA, *and Company seated at the Dais table. Court Minstrel and Court Fool sitting on the Dais step.*

Min. How gayly smile the heavens,
The light winds whisper gay;

For royal birth and knightly worth
Are knit to one to-day.

Fool [*Drowning his voice.*]

So we 'll flatter them up, and we 'll cocker them up,
Till we turn young brains;
And pamper the brach till we make her a wolf,
And get bit by the legs for our pains.

Monks [*Chanting without.*]

A fastu et superbiâ
Domine libera nos.

Min. 'Neath sandal red and samité,
Are knights and ladies set;
The henchmen tall stride through the hall,
The board with wine is wet.

Fool. Oh! merrily growls the starving hind,
At my full skin;
And merrily howl wolf, wind, and owl,
While I lie warm within.

Monks. A luxu et avaritiâ
Domine libera nos.

Min. Hark! from the bridal bower,
Rings out the bridesmaid's song;
"'Tis the mystic hour of an untried power,
The bride she tarries long."

Fool. She 's schooling herself and she 's steeling herself,
Against the dreary day,
When she 'll pine and sigh from her lattice high,
For the knight that 's far away.

Monks. A carnis illectamentis
Domine libera nos.

Min. Blest maid! fresh roses o'er thee
The careless years shall fling;
While days and nights shall new delights
To sense and fancy bring.

Fool. Satins and silks, and feathers and lace,
Will gild life's pill;
In jewels and gold folks cannot grow old,
Fine ladies will never fall ill.

Monks. A vanitatibus sæculi
Domine libera nos.

[SOPHIA *descends from the Dais, leading* ELIZABETH. *Ladies follow.*]

Soph. [*to the Fool.*] Silence, you screech-owl.
Come strew flowers, fair ladies,
And lead unto her bower our fairest bride,
The cynosure of love and beauty here,
Who shrines heaven's graces in earth's richest casket.

Eliz. I come: [*aside*] Here, Guta, take those monks a fee—
Tell them I thank them—bid them pray for me.
I am half mazed with trembling joy within,
And noisy wassail round—'tis well, for else
The spectre of my duties and my dangers
Would whelm my heart with terror. Ah! poor self!
Thou took'st this for the term and bourne of troubles—
And now 'tis here, thou findest it the gate
Of new sin-cursed infinities of labour,

Where thou must do, or die!
[*Aloud.*] Lead on. I'll follow. [*Exeunt.*

Fool. There, now. No fee for the fool; and yet my prescription was as good as those old Jeremies'. But in law, physic, and divinity, folks had sooner be poisoned in Latin, than saved in the mother-tongue.

ACT II.

SCENE I. A.D. 1221–7.

ELIZABETH'S *Bower. Night.* LEWIS *sleeping in an Alcove.* ELIZABETH *lying on the Floor in the Foreground.*

Eliz. No streak yet in the blank and eyeless east—
More weary hours to ache, and smart, and shiver
On these bare boards, within a step of bliss.
Why peevish? 'Tis mine own will keeps me here—
And yet I hate myself for that same will:
Fightings within and out! How easy 'twere, now,
Just to be like the rest, and let life run—
To use up to the rind what joys God sends us,
Not thus forestall His rod: What! and so lose
The strength which comes by suffering? Well, if grief
Be gain, mine's double—fleeing thus the snare
Of yon luxurious and unnerving down,
And widowed from mine Eden. And why widowed?
Because they tell me, love is of the flesh,
And that's our house-bred foe, the adder in our bosoms,
Which warmed to life, will sting us. They must
know ———
I do confess mine ignorance, Oh Lord!
Mine earnest will these painful limbs may prove.

* * * * * *

And yet I swore to love him.—So I do
No more than I have sworn. Am I to blame

If God makes wedlock that, which if it be not,
It were a shame for modest lips to speak it,
And silly doves are better mates than we?
And yet our love is Jesus' due,—and all things
Which share with Him divided empery
Are snares and idols—"To love, to cherish, and to obey!"

* * * * * *

Oh! deadly riddle! Rent and twofold life!
Oh! cruel troth! To keep thee or to break thee
Alike seems sin! Oh! thou beloved tempter,

[*Turning toward the bed.*

Who first didst teach me love, why on thyself
From God divert thy lesson? Wilt provoke Him?
What if mine heavenly Spouse in jealous ire
Should smite mine earthly spouse? Have I two husbands?
The words are horror—yet they are orthodox!

[*Rises and goes to the window.*

* * * * * *

How many many brows of happy lovers
The fragrant lips of night even now are kissing!
Some wandering hand in hand through arched lanes;
Some listening for loved voices at the lattice;
Some steeped in dainty dreams of untried bliss;
Some nestling soft and deep in well-known arms,
Whose touch makes sleep rich life. The very birds
Within their nests are wooing! So much love!
All seek their mates, or finding, rest in peace;

The earth seems one vast bride-bed. Doth God tempt us?
Is 't all a veil to blind our eyes from Him?
A fire-fly at the candle! 'Tis love leads him:
Love 's light, and light is love: Oh, Eden! Eden!
Eve was a virgin there, they say; God knows.
Must all this be as it had never been?
Is it all a fleeting type of higher love?
Why, if the lesson 's pure, is not the teacher
Pure also? Is it my shame to feel no shame?
Am I more clean, the more I scent uncleanness?
Shall base emotions picture Christ's embrace?
Rest, rest, torn heart! Yet where? in earth or heaven?
Still, from out the bright abysses, gleams our Lady's silver footstool,
Still the light-world sleeps beyond her, though the night-clouds fleet below.
Oh! that I were walking, far above, upon that dappled pavement,
Heaven's floor, which is the ceiling of the dungeon where we lie.
Ah, what blessed Saints might meet me, on that platform, sliding silent,
Past us in its airy travels, angel-wafted, mystical!
They perhaps might tell me all things, opening up the secret fountains
Which now struggle, dark and turbid, through their dreary prison clay.
Love! art thou an earth-born streamlet, that thou seek'st the lowest hollows?

Sure some vapours float up from thee, mingling with the highest blue.
Spirit-love in spirit-bodies, melted into one existence—
Joining praises through the ages—Is it all a minstrel's dream?
Alas! he wakes. [LEWIS *rises.*

Lew. Ah! faithless beauty,
Is this your promise, that whene'er you prayed
I should be still the partner of your vigils,
And learn from you to pray? Last night I lay dissembling
When she who woke you, took my feet for yours:
Now I shall seize my lawful prize perforce.
Alas! what's this? These shoulders' cushioned ice,
And thin soft flanks, with purple lashes all,
And weeping furrows traced! Ah! precious life-blood!
Who has done this?

Eliz. Forgive! 'twas I—my maidens—

Lew. O, ruthless hags!

Eliz. Not so, not so—They wept
When I did bid them, as I bid thee now
To think of nought but love.

Lew. Elizabeth!
Speak! I will know the meaning of this madness!

Eliz. Beloved, thou hast heard how godly souls,
In every age, have tamed the rebel flesh
By such sharp lessons. I must tread their paths,
If I would climb the mountains where they rest.
Grief is the gate of bliss—why wedlock—knighthood—

A mother's joys—a hard-earned field of glory—
By tribulation come—so doth God's kingdom.

Lew. But doleful nights, and self-inflicted tortures——
Are these the love of God? Is He well pleased
With this stern holocaust of health and joy?

Eliz. What? Am I not as gay a lady-love
As ever clipt in arms a noble knight?
Am I not blithe as bird the live-long day?
It pleases me to bear what you call pain,
Therefore to me 'tis pleasure: joy and grief
Are the will's creatures; martyrs kiss the stake—
The moorland colt enjoys the thorny furze—
The dullest boor will seek a fight, and count
His pleasure by his wounds; you must forget, love,
Eve's curse lays suffering, as their natural lot,
On womankind, till custom makes it light.
I know the use of pain; bar not the leech
Because his cure is bitter—'Tis such medicine
Which breeds that paltry strength, that weak devotion,
For which you say you love me.—Ay, which brings
Even when most sharp, a stern and awful joy
As its attendant angel—I'll say no more—
Not even to thee—command, and I'll obey thee.

Lew. Thou casket of all graces! fourfold wonder
Of wit and beauty, love and wisdom! Canst thou
Beatify the ascetic's savagery
To heavenly prudence? Horror melts to pity,
And pity kindles to adoring shower
Of radiant tears! Thou tender cruelty!

Gay smiling martyrdom! Shall I forbid thee?
Limit thy depth by mine own shallowness?
Thy courage by my weakness? Where thou darest,
I'll shudder and submit. I kneel here spell-bound
Before my bleeding Saviour's living likeness
To worship, not to cavil: I had dreamt of such things,
Dim heard in legends, while my pitiful blood
Tingled through every vein, and wept, and swore
'Twas beautiful, 'twas Christ-like—had I thought
That thou wert such:—
Eliz. You would have loved me still?
Lew. I had gone mad, I think, at every parting
At mine own terrors for thee. No; I'll learn to glory
In that which makes thee glorious! Noble stains!
I'll call them rose leaves out of paradise
Strewn on the wreathed snows, or rubies dropped
From martyrs' diadems, prints of Jesus' cross
Too truly borne, alas!
Eliz. I think, mine own,
I am forgiven at last?
Lew. To-night, my sister—
Henceforth I'll clasp thee to my heart so fast
Thou shalt not 'scape unnoticed.—
Eliz. [*laughing.*] We shall see—
Now I must stop those wise lips with a kiss,
And lead thee back to scenes of simpler bliss.

SCENE II.

A Chamber in the Castle. ELIZABETH—*the Fool*—ISENTRUDIS —GUTA *singing.*

Far among the lonely hills,
As I lay beside my sheep,
Rest came down upon my soul,
From the everlasting deep.

Changeless march the stars above,
Changeless morn succeeds to even ;
And the everlasting hills,
Changeless watch the changeless heaven.

See the rivers, how they run,
Changeless to a changeless sea ;
All around is forethought sure,
Fixed will and stern decree.

Can the sailor move the main ?
Will the potter heed the clay ?
Mortal ! where the spirit drives,
Thither must the wheels obey.

Neither ask, nor fret, nor strive :
Where thy path is, thou shalt go.
He who made the stream of time
Wafts thee down to weal or woe.

Eliz. That 's a sweet song, and yet it does not chime
With my heart's inner voice. Where had you it,
Guta?

Guta. From a nun who was a shepherdess in her youth—sadly plagued she was by a cruel step-mother, till she fled to a convent and found rest to her soul.

Fool. No doubt; nothing so pleasant as giving up one's own will in one's own way. But she might have learnt all that without taking cold on the hill-tops.

Eliz. Where then, fool?

Fool. At any market-cross where two or three rogues are together, who have neither grace to mend, nor courage to say "I did it." Now you shall see the shepherdess's baby, dressed in my cap and bells.

[*Sings.*

When I was a greenhorn and young,
And wanted to be and to do,
I puzzled my brains about choosing my line,
Till I found out the way that things go.

The same piece of clay makes a tile,
A pitcher, a taw, or a brick:
Dan Horace knew life; you may cut out a saint,
Or a bench from the self-same stick.

The urchin who squalls in a jail,
By circumstance turns out a rogue;
While the castle-born brat is a senator born,
Or a saint, if religion 's in vogue.

We fall on our legs in this world,
Blind kittens, tossed in neck and heels:
'Tis dame Circumstance licks Nature's cubs into
shape,
She 's the mill-head, if we are the wheels.

Then why puzzle and fret, plot and dream?
He that 's wise will just follow his nose;
Contentedly fish, while he swims with the stream;
'Tis no business of his where it goes.

Eliz. Far too well sung for such a saucy song.
So go.

Fool. Ay, I'll go. Whip the dog out of church, and then rate him for being no Christian. [*Exit* FOOL.

Eliz. Guta, there is sense in that knave's ribaldry:
We must not thus baptize our idleness,
And call it resignation: Which is love?
To do God's will, or merely suffer it?
I do not love that contemplative life:
No! I must headlong into seas of toil,
Leap forth from self, and spend my soul on others.
Oh! contemplation palls upon the spirit,
Like the chill silence of an autumn sun:
While action, like the roaring southwest wind,
Sweeps laden with elixirs, with rich draughts
Quickening the wombed earth.

Guta. And yet what bliss,
When, dying in the darkness of God's light,

The soul can pierce these blinding webs of nature,
And float up to The Nothing, which is all things—
The ground of being, where self-forgetful silence
Is emptiness,—emptiness fulness,—fulness God,—
Till we touch Him, and like a snow-flake, melt
Upon His light-sphere's keen circumference!

Eliz. Hast thou felt this?

Guta. In part.

Eliz. Oh, happy Guta!
Mine eyes are dim—and what if I mistook
For God's own self, the phantoms of my brain?
And who am I, that my own will's intent
Should put me face to face with the living God?
I, thus thrust down from the still lakes of thought
Upon a boiling crater-field of labour.
No! He must come to me, not I to Him;
If I see God, beloved, I must see Him
In mine own self:—

Guta. Thyself?

Eliz. Why start, my sister?
God is revealed in the crucified:
The crucified must be revealed in me:—
I must put on His righteousness; show forth
His sorrow's glory; hunger, weep with Him;
Writhe with His stripes, and let this aching flesh
Sink through His fiery baptism into death,
That I may rise with Him, and in his likeness
May ceaseless heal the sick, and soothe the sad,
And give away like Him this flesh and blood

To feed His lambs—ay—we must die with Him
To sense—and love—

Guta. To love? What, then, becomes
Of marriage vows?

Eliz. I know it—so speak not of them.
Oh! that 's the flow, the chasm in all my longings,
Which I have spanned with cobweb arguments,
Yet yawns before me still, where'er I turn,
To bar me from perfection; had I given
My virgin all to Christ! I was not worthy!
I could not stand alone!

Guta. Here comes your husband.

Eliz. He comes! my sun! and every thrilling vein
Proclaims my weakness. [LEWIS *enters.*

Lew. Good news, my princess; in the street below
Conrad, the man of God from Marpurg, stands,
And from a bourne-stone to the simple folk
Does thunder doctrine, preaching faith, repentance,
And dread of all foul heresies; his eyes
On heaven still set, save when with searching frown
He lours upon the crowd, who round him cower
Like quails beneath the hawk, and gape, and tremble,
Now raised to heaven, now down again to hell.
I stood beside and heard; like any doe's
My heart did rise and fall.

Eliz. Oh, let us hear him!
We too need warning; shame, if we let pass
Unentertained, God's angels on their way.
Send for him, brother.

Lew. Let a knight go down
And say to the holy man, the Landgrave Lewis
With humble greetings prays his blessedness
To make these secular walls the spirit's temple
At least to-night.
Eliz. Now go, my ladies, both—
Prepare fit lodgings,—let your courtesies
Retain in our poor courts the man of God.
[*Exeunt.* LEWIS *and* ELIZABETH *are left alone.*
Now hear me, best-beloved: I have marked this man:
And that which hath scared others, draws me towards him:
He has the graces which I want; his sternness
I envy for its strength; his fiery boldness
I call the earnestness which dares not trifle
With life's huge stake; his coldness but the calm
Of one who long hath found, and keeps unwavering,
Clear purpose still; he hath the gift which speaks
The deepest things most simply; in his eye
I dare be happy—weak I dare not be.
With such a guide,—to save this little heart—
The burden of self-rule—Oh—half my work
Were eased, and I could live for thee and thine,
And take no thought of self. Oh, be not jealous,
Mine own, mine idol! For thy sake I ask it—
I would but be a mate and help more meet
For all thy knightly virtues.
Lew. 'Tis too true!
I have felt it long; we stand, two weakling children,

Under too huge a burden, while temptations
Like adders swarm up round: I must be led—
But thou alone shalt lead me.

Eliz. I? beloved!
This load more? Strengthen, Lord, the feeble knees!

Lew. Yes! thou, my queen, who making thyself once mine,
Hast made me sevenfold thine; I own thee guide
Of my devotions, mine ambition's loadstar,
The Saint whose shrine I serve with lance and lute;
If thou wilt have a ruler, let him be
Through thee, the ruler of thy slave. [*Kneels to her.*

Eliz. Oh, kneel not—
But grant my prayer—If we shall find this man,
As well I know him, worthy, let him be
Director of my conscience and my actions
With all but thee—Within love's inner shrine
We shall be still alone—But joy! here comes
Our embassy, successful.

Enter CONRAD, *with* COUNT WALTER, *Monks, Ladies, &c.*

Con. Peace to this house.

Eliz. Hail to your holiness.

Lew. The odour of your sanctity and might
With balmy steam, and gales of Paradise
Forestalls you hither.

Eliz. Bless us doubly, master,
With holy doctrine, and with holy prayers.

Con. Children, I am the servant of Christ's servants—

And needs must yield to those who may command
By right of creed; I do accept your bounty—
Not for myself, but for that priceless name,
Whose dread authority and due commission,
Attested by the seal of His vicegerent,
I bear unworthy here; through my vile lips
Christ and His vicar thank you; on myself—
And these, my brethren, Christ's adopted poor—
A menial's crust, and some waste nook, or dog-hutch,
Wherein the worthless flesh may nightly hide,
Are best bestowed.

Eliz. You shall be where you will—
Do what you will; unquestioned, unobserved,
Enjoy, refrain; silence and solitude,
The better part which such like spirits choose,
We will provide; only be you our master,
And we your servants, for a few short days:
Oh, blessed days!

Con. Ah, be not hasty, madam!
Think whom you welcome; one who has no skill
To wink and speak smooth things; whom fear of God
Constrains to daily wrath; who brings, alas!
A sword, not peace; within whose bones the word
Burns like a pent-up fire, and makes him bold
If aught in you or yours shall seem amiss,
To cry aloud and spare not; let me go—
To pray for you—as I have done long time,
Is sweeter than to chide you.

Eliz. Then your prayers

Shall drive home your rebukes; for both we need you—
Our snares are many, and our sins are more.
So say not nay—I'll speak with you apart.

[ELIZABETH *and* CONRAD *retire.*

Lew. [*aside.*] Well, Walter, mine, how like you the good legate?

Wal. Walter has seen nought of him but his eye;
And that don't please him.

Lew. How so, sir! that face
Is pure and meek—a calm and thoughtful eye.

Wal. A shallow, stony, steadfast eye; that looks at neither man nor beast in the face, but at something invisible a yard before him, through you and past you, at a fascination, a ghost of fixed purposes that haunts him, from which neither reason nor pity will turn him. I have seen such an eye in men possessed—with devils, or with self: sleek passionless men, who are too refined to be manly, and measure their grace by their effeminacy; crooked vermin, who swarm up in pious times, being drowned out of their earthy haunts by the spring-tide of religion; and so making a gain of godliness, swim upon the first of the flood, till it cast them ashore on the firm beach of wealth and station. I always mistrust those wall-eyed saints.

Lew. Beware, sir Count, your keen and worldly wit
Is good for worldly uses, not to tilt
Withal at holy men and holy things.
He pleases well the spiritual sense
Of my most peerless lady, whose discernment

Is still the touchstone of my grosser fancy:
He is her friend, and mine; and you must love him
Even for our sakes alone.

[*To a bystander.*] A word with you, sir.

[*In the mean time* ELIZABETH *and* CONRAD *are talking together.*]

Eliz. I would be taught—

Con. It seems you claim some knowledge,
By choosing thus your teacher.

Eliz. I would know more—

Con. Go then to the schools—and be no wiser, madam;
And let God's charge here run to waste, to seek
The bitter fruit of knowledge—hunt the rainbow
O'er hill and dale, while wisdom rusts at home.

Eliz. I would be holy, master—

Con. Be so, then.
God's will stands fair: 'tis thine which fails, if any.

Eliz. I would know how to rule—

Con. Then must thou learn
The needs of subjects, and be ruled thyself.
Sink, if thou longest to rise; become most small—
The strength which comes by weakness makes thee great.

Eliz. I will.

Lew. What, still at lessons? Come, my fairest sister,
Usher the holy man unto his lodgings. [*Exeunt.*

Wal. [*alone.*] So, so, the birds are limed:—Heaven grant that we do not soon see them stowed in separate cages. Well, here my prophesying ends. I shall go to my lands, and see how much the gentlemen, my neighbours, have stolen off them the last week,—Priests? Frogs in the king's bedchamber! What says the song?

I once had a hound, a right good hound,
A hound both fleet and strong:
He eat at my board, and he slept by my bed,
And ran with me all the day long.

But my wife took a priest, a shaveling priest,
And "such friendships are carnal," quoth he.
So my wife and her priest they drugged the poor
beast
And the rat's-bane is waiting for me.

SCENE III.

The Gateway of a Convent. Night. Enter CONRAD.

Con. This night she swears obedience to me!
Wondrous Lord!
How hast Thou opened a path, where my young dreams
May find fulfilment: there are prophecies
Upon her, make me bold. Why comes she not?
She should be here by now. Strange, how I shrink—
I, who ne'er yet felt fear of man or fiend.
Obedience to my will! An awful charge!
But yet, to have the training of her sainthood;
To watch her rise above this wild world's waves
Like floating water-lily, towards heaven's light
Opening its virgin snows, with golden eye
Mirroring the golden sun; to be her champion,

And war with fiends for her; that were a "quest"—
That were true chivalry; to bring my Judge
This jewel for His crown; this noble soul,
Worth thousand prudish clods of barren clay,
Who mope for heaven because earth's grapes are sour—
Her, full of youth, flushed with the heart's rich first-fruits,
Tangled in earthly pomp—and earthly love.
Wife? Saint by her face she should be: with such looks
The queen of heaven, perchance, slow pacing came
Adown our sleeping wards, when Dominic
Sank fainting, drunk with beauty:—she is most fair!
Pooh! I know nought of fairness—this I know,
She calls herself my slave, with such an air
As speaks her queen, not slave; that shall be looked to—
She must be pinioned, or she will range abroad
Upon too bold a wing; 'twill cost her pain—
But what of that? there are worse things than pain—
What! not yet here? I'll in, and there await her
In prayer before the altar; I have need on't:
And shall have more before this harvest 's ripe.

As CONRAD *goes out*, ELIZABETH, ISENTRUDIS, *and* GUTA *enter.*

Eliz. I saw him just before us: let us onward
We must not seem to loiter.
Isen. Then you promise
Exact obedience to his sole direction
Henceforth in every scruple?

Eliz. In all I can,
And be a wife.

Guta. Is it not a double bondage?
A husband's will is clog enough. Be sure,
Though free, I crave more freedom.

Eliz. So do I—
This servitude shall free me—from myself.
Therefore I'll swear.

Isen. To what?

Eliz. I know not wholly:
But this I know, that I shall swear to-night
To yield my will unto a wiser will;
To see God's truth through eyes, which, like the eagle's,
From higher Alps undazzled eye the sun.
Compelled to discipline from which my sloth
Would shrink, unbidden,—to deep devious paths
Which my dull sight would miss, I now can plunge,
And dare life's eddies fearless.

Isen. You will repent it.

Eliz. I do repent, even now. Therefore I'll swear—
And bind myself to that, which once being right,
Will not be less right, when I shrink from it.
No; if the end be gained—if I be raised
To freer, nobler use, I'll dare, I'll welcome
Him and his means, though they were racks and flames.
Come, ladies, let us in, and to the chapel. [*Exeunt*

SCENE IV.

A Chamber. GUTA, ISENTRUDIS, *and a Lady.*

Lady. Doubtless she is most holy—but for wisdom—
Say if 'tis wise to spurn all rules, all censures,
And mountebank it in the public ways
Till she becomes a jest?
Isen. How 's this?
Lady. For one thing—
Yestreen I passed her in the open street,
Following the vocal line of chanting priests,
Clad in rough serge, and with her bare soft palms
Wooing the ruthless flints; the gaping crowd
Unknowing whom they held, did thrust and jostle
Her tender limbs; she saw me as she passed—
And blushed and veiled her face, and smiled withal.
Isen. Oh, think, she 's not seventeen yet.
Guta. Why expect
Wisdom with love in all? Each has his gift—
Our souls are organ pipes of diverse stop
And various pitch; each with its proper notes
Thrilling beneath the self-same breath of God.
Though poor alone, yet joined, they 're harmony.
Besides, these higher spirits must not bend
To common methods; in their inner world
They move by broader laws, at whose expression
We must adore, not cavil: here she comes—
The ministering Saint, fresh from the poor of Christ.

ELIZABETH *enters without cloak or shoes, carrying an empty basket.*

Isen. What 's here, my princess? Guta, fetch her robes!
Rest, rest, my child!

Eliz. [*Throwing herself on a seat.*] Oh! I have seen such things!
I shudder still; your bright looks dazzle me;
As those who long in hideous darkness pent
Blink at the daily light; this room 's too gay!
We sit in a cloud, and sing, like pictured angels,
And say, the world runs smooth—while right below
Welters the black, fermenting heap of life
On which our state is built: I saw this day
What we might be, and still be Christian women:
And mothers too—I saw one, laid in childbed
These three cold weeks upon the black damp straw;
No nurses, cordials, or that nice parade
With which we try to balk the curse of Eve—
And yet she laughed, and showed her buxom boy,
And said, Another week, so please the Saints,
She 'd be at work a-field. Look here—and here—
[*Pointing round the room.*
I saw no such things there; and yet they lived.
Our wanton accidents take root, and grow
To vaunt themselves God 's laws, until our clothes,
Our gems, and gaudy books, and cushioned litters
Become ourselves, and we would fain forget
There live who need them not. [GUTA *offers to robe her.*

Let be, beloved—
I will taste somewhat this same poverty—
Try these temptations, grudges, gnawing shames,
For which 'tis blamed; how probe an unfelt evil?
Would'st be the poor man's friend? Must freeze with him—
Test sleepless hunger—let thy crippled back
Ache o'er the endless furrow; how was He,
The blessed One, made perfect? Why, by grief—
The fellowship of voluntary grief—
He read the tear-stained book of poor men's souls,
As I must learn to read it. Lady! lady!
Wear but one robe the less—forego one meal—
And thou shalt taste the core of many tales
Which now flit past thee, like a minstrel's songs,
The sweeter for their sadness.—

Lady. Heavenly wisdom!
Forgive me!

Eliz. How? What wrong is mine, fair dame?

Lady. I thought you, to my shame—less wise than holy.
But you have conquered: I will test these sorrows
On mine own person; I have toyed too long
In painted pinnace down the stream of life,
Witched with the landscape, while the weary rowers
Faint at the groaning oar: I'll be thy pupil.
Farewell. Heaven bless thy labours and thy lesson. [*Exit.*

Isen. We are alone. Now tell me, dearest lady,
How came you in this plight?

Eliz. Oh! chide not, nurse—

My heart is full—and yet I went not far—
Even here, close by, where my own bower looks down
Upon that unknown sea of wavy roofs,
I turned into an alley 'neath the wall—
And stepped from earth to hell.—The light of heaven,
The common air, was narrow, gross, and dun;
The tiles did drop from the eaves; the unhinged doors
Tottered o'er inky pools, where reeked and curdled
The offal of a life; the gaunt-haunched swine
Growled at their christened playmates o'er the scraps.
Shrill mothers cursed; wan children wailed; sharp coughs
Rang through the crazy chambers; hungry eyes
Glared dumb reproach, and old perplexity,
Too stale for words; o'er still and webless looms
The listless craftsmen through their elf-locks scowled;
These were my people! all I had, I gave—
They snatched it thankless; (was it not their own?
Wrung from their veins, returning all too late?)
Or in the new delight of rare possession,
Forgot the giver; one did sit apart,
And shivered on a stone; beneath her rags
Nestled two impish, fleshless, leering boys,
Grown old before their youth; they cried for bread—
She chid them down, and hid her face and wept;
I had given all—I took my cloak, my shoes,
(What could I else? 'Twas but a moment's want
Which she had borne, and borne day after day,)
And clothed her bare gaunt arms and purpled feet,
Then slunk ashamed away to wealth and honour.

CONRAD *enters.*

What? Conrad? unannounced! This is too bold!
Peace! I have lent myself—and I must take
The usury of that loan: your pleasure, master?

Con. Madam, but yesterday, I bade your presence,
To hear the preached word of God; I preached—
And yet you came not—Where is now your oath?
Where is the right to bid, you gave to me?
Am I your ghostly guide? I asked it not.
Of your own will you tendered that, which, given,
Became not choice, but duty.—What is here?
Think not that alms, or lowly-seeming garments,
Self-willed humilities, pride's decent mummers,
Can raise above obedience; she from God
Her sanction draws, while these we forge ourselves,
Mere tools to clear her necessary path.
Go free—thou art no slave: God doth not own
Unwilling service, and His ministers
Must lure, not drag in leash; henceforth I leave thee:
Riot in thy self-willed fancies; pick thy steps
By thine own will-o'-the-wisp toward the pit;
Farewell, proud girl. [*Exit.* CONRAD.

Eliz. Oh God! What have I done?
I have cast off the clue of this world's maze,
And like an idiot, let my boat adrift
Above the water-fall!—I had no message—
How 's this?

Isen. We passed it by, as matter of no moment
Upon the sudden coming of your guests.

Eliz. No moment! 'Tis enough to have driven him forth—
And that's enough to damn me: I'll not chide you—
I can see nothing but my loss; I'll to him—
I'll go in sackcloth, bathe his feet with tears—
And know nor sleep nor food till I am forgiven—
And you must with me, ladies. Come and find him.
[*Exeunt.*

SCENE V.

A Hall in the Castle. In the background a Group of diseased and deformed Beggars; CONRAD *entering,* ELIZABETH *comes forward to meet him.*

Con. What dost thou, daughter?
Eliz. Ah, my honoured master!
That name speaks pardon, sure.
Con. What dost thou, daughter?
Eliz. I have been washing these poor people's feet.
Con. A wise humiliation.
Eliz. So I meant it—
And use it as a penance for my pride;
And yet, alas, through my own vulgar likings
Or stubborn self-conceit, 'tis none to me.
I marvel how the Saints thus tamed their spirits:
Sure to be humbled by such toil, but proves,
Not cures, our lofty mind.
Con. Thou speakest well—
The knave who serves unto another's needs
Knows himself abler than the man who needs him;

And she who stoops, will not forget, that stooping
Implies a height to stoop from.
Eliz. Could I see
My Saviour in His poor!
Con. Thou shalt hereafter:
But now to wash Christ's feet were dangerous honour
For weakling grace; would you be humble, daughter,
You must look up, not down, and see yourself
A paltry atom, sap-transmitting vein
Of Christ's vast vine; the pettiest joint and member
Of His great body; own no strength, no will,
Save that which from the ruling head's command
Through me, as nerve, derives; let thyself die—
And dying, rise again to fuller life.
To be a whole is to be small and weak—
To be a part is to be great and mighty
In the one spirit of the mighty whole—
The spirit of the martyrs and the saints—
The spirit of the queen, on whose towered neck
We hang, blest ringlets!
Eliz. Why! thine eyes flash fire!
Con. But hush! such words are not for courts and halls—
Alone with God and me, thou shalt hear more.
[*Exit* CONRAD
Eliz. As when rich chanting ceases suddenly—
And the rapt sense collapses!—Oh, that Lewis
Could feed my soul thus! But to work—to work—
What wilt thou, little maid? Ah, I forgot thee—
The mother lies in childbed—Say, in time

I'll bring the baby to the font myself.
It knits them unto me, and me to them,
That bond of sponsorship—How now, good dame—
Whence then so sad?

Woman. An 't please your nobleness,
My neighbour Gretl is with her husband laid
In burning fever.

Eliz. I will come to them.

Woman. Alack, the place is foul for such as you;
And fear of plague has cleared the lane of lodgers;
If you could send—

Eliz. What? where I am afraid
To go myself, send others? That 's strange doctrine.
I'll be with you anon. [*Goes up into the Hall.*

ISENTRUDIS *enters with a basket.*

Isen. Why, here 's a weight—These cordials now, and simples,
Want a stout page to bear them; yet her fancy
Is still to go alone, to help herself.—
Where will 't all end? In madness, or the grave?
No limbs can stand these drudgeries; no spirit
The fretting harrow which this ruffian priest
Calls education—
Ah! here comes our Count.

[COUNT WALTER *enters as from a journey.*]

Too late, sir, and too seldom—Where have you been
These four months past, while we are sold for bond-slaves
Unto a peevish friar?

Wal. Why, my fair rose-bud—
A trifle overblown, but not less sweet—
I have been pining for you, till my hair
Is as gray as any badger's.

Isen. I'll not jest.

Wal. What? has my wall-eyed Saint shown you his temper?

Isen. The first of his peevish fancies was, that she should eat nothing which was not honestly and peaceably come by.

Wal. Why, I heard that you too had joined that sect.

Isen. And more fool I. But ladies are bound to set an example—while they are not bound to ask where every thing comes from: with her, poor child, scruples and starvation were her daily diet; meal after meal she rose from table empty, unless the Landgrave nodded and winked her to some lawful eatable; till she that used to take her food like an angel, without knowing it, was thinking from morning to night whether she might eat this, that, or the other.

Wal. Poor Eves! if the world leaves you innocent, the Church will not. Between the devil and the director, you are sure to get your share of the apples of knowledge!

Isen. True enough. She complained to Conrad of her scruples, and he told her, that by the law was the knowledge of sin.

Wal. But what said Lewis?

Isen. As much bewitched as she, sir. He has told her, and more than her, that were it not for the laughter and ill-will of his barons, he would join her in the same abstinence. But all this is child 's play, to the friar 's last outbreak.

Wal. Ah! The sermon which you all forgot, when the Marchioness of Misnia came suddenly? I heard that war had been proclaimed on that score; but what terms of peace were concluded?

Isen. Terms of peace? Do you call it peace to be delivered over to his nuns' tender mercies, myself and Guta, as well as our lady,—as if we had been bond-slaves and blackamoors?

Wal. You need not have submitted.

Isen. What? could I bear to see my poor child wandering up and down, wringing her hands like a mad woman—I who have lived for no one else this sixteen years? Guta talked sentiment,—called it a glorious cross, and so forth.—I took it as it came.

Wal. And got no quarter, I'll warrant.

Isen. Don't talk of it—my poor back tingles at the thought!

Wal. The sweet saints think every woman of the world no better than she should be; and without meaning to be envious, owe you all a grudge for past flirtations. As I am a knight, now it 's over, I like you all the better for it.

Isen. What?

Wal. When I see a woman who will stand by her word, and two who will stand by their mistress. And the monk, too—there 's mettle in him. I took him for a canting carpet-haunter; but be sure, the man who will bully his own patrons, has an honest purpose in him, though it bears strange fruit on this wicked hither-side of the grave. Now, my fair nymph of the birchen-tree, use your interest to find me supper and lodging; for your elegant squires of the trencher look surly on me here: I am the prophet who has no honour in his own country.

[*Exeunt.*

SCENE VI.

Dawn. A rocky path leading to a mountain Chapel. A Peasant sitting on a stone with dog and Crossbow.

Peasant singing.

Over the wild moor, in reddest dawn of morning,
Gayly the huntsman down green droves must roam:
Over the wild moor, in grayest wane of evening,
Weary the huntsman comes wandering home;
Home, home,

If he has one. Who comes here?

[*A Woodcutter enters with a laden ass.*]

What art going about?

Woodcutter. To warm other folks' backs.

Peas. Thou art in the common lot—Jack earns and Gill spends—therein lies the true division of labour. What 's thy name?

Woodc. Be'est a keeper, man, or a charmer, that dost so catechize me?

Peas. Both—I am a keeper, for I keep all I catch; and a charmer, for I drive bad spirits out of honest men's turnips.

Woodc. Mary sain us, what be they like?

Peas. Four-legged kitchens of leather, cooking farmers' crops into butcher's meat by night, without leave or license.

Woodc. By token, thou 'rt a deer stealer?

Peas. Stealer, quoth he? I have dominion. I do what I like with mine own.

Woodc. Thine own?

Peas. Yea, marry—for saith the priest, man has dominion over the beast of the field and the fowl of the air: so I, being as I am a man, as men go, have dominion over the deer in my trade, as you have in yours over sleep-mice and woodpeckers.

Woodc. Then every man has a right to be a poacher.

Peas. Every man has his gift, and the tools go to him that can use them. Some are born workmen; some have souls above work. I'm one of that metal. I was meant to own land and do nothing; but the angel that deals out babies' souls, mistook the cradles, and spoilt a gallant gentleman! Well—I forgive him! there were many born the same night—and work wears the wits.

Woodc. I had sooner draw in a yoke than hunt in a halter. Had'st best repent and mend thy ways.

Peas. The way-warden may do that: I wear out no ways, I go across country. Mend? saith he? Why I can but starve at worst, or groan with the rheumatism, which you do already. And who would reek and wallow o' nights in the same straw, like a stalled cow, when he may have his choice of all the clean holly bushes in the forest?

Who would grub out his life in the same croft, when he has free-warren of all fields between this and Rhine? Not I. I have dirtied my share of spades myself; but I slipped my leash and went self-hunting.

Woodc. But what if thou be caught and brought up before the prince?

Peas. He don't care for game. He has put down his kennel, and keeps a tame saint instead; and when I am driven in, I shall ask my pardon of her in St. John's name. They say that for his sake she 'll give away the shoes off her feet.

Woodc. I would not stand in your shoes for all the top and lop in the forest. Murder! Here comes a ghost! Run up the bank—shove the jackass into the ditch.

[*A white figure comes up the path with lights.*]

Peas. A ghost or a watchman, and one 's as bad as the other—so we may take to cover for the time.

[ELIZABETH *enters meanly clad, carrying her new-born infant;* ISENTRUDIS *following with a taper and gold pieces on a salver.* ELIZABETH *passes, singing.*]

Deep in the warm vale the village is sleeping,
Sleeping the firs on the bleak rock above;
Nought wakes, save grateful hearts, silently creeping
Up to their Lord in the might of their love.

What Thou hast given to me, Lord, here I bring Thee,
Odour, and light, and the magic of gold;

Feet which must follow Thee, lips which must sing
Thee,
Limbs which must ache for Thee ere they grow
old.

What Thou hast given to me, Lord, here I tender,
Life of mine own life, the fruit of my love;
Take him, yet leave him me, till I shall render
Count of the precious charge, kneeling above.

[*They pass up the path. The peasants come out.*]

Peas. No ghost, but a mighty pretty wench, with a mighty sweet voice.

Woodc. Wench, indeed! Where be thy manners? 'Tis her Ladyship—the Princess.

Peas. The Princess! Ay, I thought those little white feet were but lately out of broadcloth—still, I say, a mighty sweet voice—I wish she had not sung so sweetly—it makes things to arise in a body's head, does that singing: a wonderful handsome lady! a royal lady!

Woodc. But a most unwise one. Did ye mind the gold? If I had such a trencher full, it should sleep warm in a stocking, instead of being made a brother to owls here, for every rogue to snatch at.

Peas. Why then? who dare harm such as her, man?

Woodc. Nay, nay, none of us, we are poor folks, we fear God and the king. But if she had met a gentleman now—heaven help her! Ah! thou has lost a chance—thou might'st have run out promiscuously, and down on thy knees, and begged thy pardon for the new comer's sake. There was a chance, indeed.

Peas. Pooh, man, I have done nothing but lose chances all my days. I fell into the fire the day I was christened, and ever since I am like a fresh-trimmed fir-tree; every foul feather sticks to me.

Woodc. Go, shrive thyself, and the priest will scrub off thy turpentine with a new haircloth; and now, good day, the maids are a-waiting for their firewood.

Peas. A word before you go—Take warning by me—Avoid that same serpent, wisdom—Pray to the Saints to make you a blockhead—Never send your boys to school—For Heaven knows, a poor man that will live honest, and die in his bed, ought to have no more scholarship than a parson, and no more brains than your jackass.

SCENE VII.

The Gateway of a Castle. ELIZABETH *and her suite standing at the top of a flight of steps. Mob below.*

Peas. Bread! Bread! Bread! give us bread; we perish.

1*st Voice.* Ay, give, give, give! God knows we 're long past earning.

2*d Voice.* Our skeleton children lie along in the roads—

3*d Voice.* Our sheep drop dead about the frozen leas—

4*th Voice.* Our harness and our shoes are boiled for food—

Old Man's Voice. Starved, withered, autumn hay that thanks the scythe!
Send out your swordsmen, mow the dry bents down,
And make this long death short—we 'll never struggle.

All. Bread, bread!

Eliz. Ay, bread—Where is it knights and servants?
Why butler, seneschal, this food forthcomes not?

Butler. Alas, we 've eaten all ourselves: heaven knows
The pages broke the buttery hatches down—
The boys were starved almost.

Voice below. Ay, she can find enough to feast her minions.

Woman's Voice. How can she know what 'tis, for months and months
To stoop and straddle in the clogging fallows,
Bearing about a living babe within you?
And then at night to fat yourself and it
On fir-bark, madam, and water.

Eliz. My good dame—
That which you bear, I bear: for food, God knows,
I have not tasted food this livelong day—
Nor will, till you are served. I sent for wheat,
From Köln and from the Rhine-land days ago,
Oh God! why comes it not?

Enter from below COUNT WALTER, *with a Merchant.*

Wal. Stand back; you 'll choke me, rascals:
Archers, bring up those mules. Here comes the corn—
Here comes your guardian angel, plenty-laden,

With no white wings, but good white wheat, my boys,
Quarters on quarters—if you 'll pay for it.

Eliz. Oh! give him all he asks.

Wal. The scoundrel wants
Three times its value.

Merchant. Not a penny less—
I bought it on speculation—I must live—
I get my bread by buying corn that 's cheap,
And selling where 'tis dearest. Mass, you need it,
And you must pay according to your need.

Mob. Hang him! hang all regraters—hang the forestalling dog!

Wal. Driver, lend here the halter off that mule.

Eliz. Nay, Count; the corn is his, and his the right
To fix conditions for his own.

Mer. Well spoken!
A wise and royal lady! She will see
The trade protected. Why, I kept the corn
Three months on venture. Now, so help me Saints,
I am a loser by it, quite a loser—
So help me Saints, I am.

Eliz. You will not sell it
Save at a price, which, by the bill you tender,
Is far beyond our means. Heaven knows, I grudge not—
I have sold my plate, have pawned my robes and jewels,
Mortgaged broad lands and castles to buy food—
And now I have no more—Abate, or trust
Our honour for the difference.

Mer. Not a penny—
I trust no nobles. I must make my profit—
I'll have my price, or take it back again.

Eliz. Most miserable, cold, short-sighted man,
Who for thy selfish gains dost welcome make
God's wrath, and battenest on thy fellows' woes,
What! wilt thou turn from heaven's gate, open to thee,
Through which thy charity may passport be,
And win thy long greed's pardon? Oh, for once
Dare to be great; show mercy to thyself!
See how that boiling sea of human heads
Waits open-mouthed to bless thee: speak the word,
And their triumphant quire of jubilation
Shall pierce God's cloudy floor with praise and prayers,
And drown the accuser's count in angels' ears.

[*In the mean time* WALTER, *&c., have been throwing down the wheat to the Mob.*]

Mob. God bless the good Count!—Bless the holy princess—
Hurrah for wheat—Hurrah for one full stomach.

Mer. Ah! that's my wheat! treason, my wheat, my money!

Eliz. Where is the wretch's wheat?

Wal. Below, my lady;
We counted on the charm of your sweet words,
And so did for him, what, your sermon ended,
He would have done himself.

Knight. 'Twere rude to doubt it.

Mer. Ye rascal barons!

What! Are we burghers monkeys for your pastime?
We'll clear the odds. [*Seizes* WALTER.

Wal. Soft, friend!—a worm will turn.

Voices below. Throw him down!

Wal. Dost hear that, friend?
Those pups are keen-toothed; they have eat of late
Worse bacon to their bread than thee. Come, come,
Put up thy knife; we'll give thee market-price—
And if thou must have more—why take it out
In board and lodging in the castle dungeon.

[WALTER *leads him out; the Mob, &c., disperse.*

Eliz. Now then—there's many a one lies faint at home—
I'll go to them myself.

Isen. What now? start forth
In this most bitter frost, so thinly clad?

Eliz. Tut, tut, I wear my working dress to-day,
And those who work, robe lightly—

Isen. Nay, my child,
For once keep up your rank.

Eliz. Then I had best
Roll to their door in lacqueyed equipage,
And dole my halfpence from a satin purse—
I am their sister—I must look like one.
I am their queen—I'll prove myself the greatest
By being the minister of all. So come—
Now to my pastime. [*Aside.*]
And in happy toil
Forget this whirl of doubt—We are weak, we are weak,

Only when still—put thou thine hand to the plough,
The spirit drives thee on.

Isen. You live too fast!

Eliz. Too fast? We live too slow—our gummy blood
Without fresh purging airs from heaven, would choke
Slower and slower, till it stopped and froze.
God! fight we not within a cursed world,
Whose very air teems thick with leagued fiends—
Each word we speak has infinite effects—
Each soul we pass must go to heaven or hell—
And this our one chance through eternity
To drop and die, like dead leaves in the brake,
Or like the meteor stone, though whelmed itself,
Kindle the dry moors into fruitful blaze—
And yet we live too fast!
Be earnest, earnest, earnest; mad, if thou wilt:
Do what thou dost as if the stake were heaven,
And that thy last deed ere the judgment-day.
When all's done, nothing's done. There's rest above—
Below let work be death, if work be love!

[*Exeunt.*

SCENE VIII.

A Chamber in the Castle. Counts WALTER, HUGO, *&c., Abbot, and Knights.*

Count Hugo. I can't forget it, as I am a Christian man. To ask for a stoup of beer at breakfast, and be told, there was no beer allowed in the house—her Ladyship had given all the malt to the poor.

Abbot. To give away the staff of life, eh?

C. Hugo. The life itself, sir, the life itself. All that barley, that would have warmed many an honest fellow's coppers, wasted in filthy cakes.

Abbot. The parent of seraphic ale degraded into plebeian dough! Indeed, sir, we have no right to lessen wantonly the amount of human enjoyment!

C. Wal. In heaven's name, what would you have her do, while the people were eating grass?

C. Hugo. Nobody asked them to eat it; nobody asked them to be there to eat it; if they will breed like rabbits, let them feed like rabbits, say I—I never married till I could keep a wife.

Abbot. Ah, Count Walter! How sad to see a man of your sense so led away by his feelings! Had but this dispensation been left to work itself out, and evolve the blessing implicit in all heaven's chastenings! Had but the stern benevolences of providence remained undisturbed by her ladyship's carnal tenderness—what a boon had this famine been!

C. Wal. How then, man?

Abbot. How many a poor soul would have been lying —Ah, blessed thought!—in Abraham's bosom; who must now toil on still in this vale of tears!—Pardon this pathetic dew—I cannot but feel as a Churchman.

3d Count. Look at it in this way, sir. There are too many of us—too many—Where you have one job you have three workmen. Why, I threw three hundred acres into pasture myself this year—it saves money, and risk, and trouble, and tithes.

C. Wal. What would you say to the Princess, who talks of breaking up all her parks to wheat next year?

3d Count. Ask her to take on the thirty families, who were just going to tramp off those three hundred acres into the Rhine-land, if she had not kept them in both senses this winter, and left them on my hands—once beggars, always beggars.

C. Hugo. Well, I'm a practical man, and I say, the sharper the famine, the higher are prices, and the higher I sell, the more I can spend; so the money circulates, sir, that's the word—like water—sure to run downwards again; and so it's as broad as it's long; and here's a health—if there was any beer—to the farmer's friends, "A bloody war and a wet harvest."

Abbot. Strongly put, though correctly. For the self-interest of each it is, which produces in the aggregate the happy equilibrium of all.

C. Wal. Well—the world is right well made, that's certain; and He who made the Jews' sin our salvation may bring plenty out of famine, and comfort out of covetousness. But look you, sirs, private selfishness may be public weal, and yet private selfishness be just as surely damned, for all that.

3d Count. I hold, sir, that every alms is a fresh badge of slavery.

C. Wal. I don't deny it.

3d Count. Then teach them independence.

C. Wal. How? By tempting them to turn thieves, when begging fails? By keeping their stomachs just at desperation-point? By starving them out here, to march off, starving all the way, to some town, in search of employment, of which, if they find it, they know no more than my horse? Likely! No, sir, to make men of them, put them not out of the reach, but out of the need of charity.

3d Count. And how, prithee? By teaching them, like our fair Landgravine, to open their mouths for all that drops? Thuringia is become a kennel of beggars in her hands.

C. Wal. In hers? In ours, sir!

Abbot. Idleness, sir, deceit, and immorality, are the three children of this same barbarous self-indulgence in alms-giving. Leave the poor alone. Let want teach them the need of self-exertion, and misery prove the foolishness of crime.

C. Wal. How? Teach them to become men by leaving them brutes?

Abbot. Oh, sir, there we step in, with the consolations and instructions of the faith.

C. Wal. Ay, but while the grass is growing the steed is starving; and in the mean time, how will the callow chick Grace, stand against the tough old game-cock, Hunger?

3d Count. Then how, in the name of patience, would you have us alter things?

C. Wal. We cannot alter them, sir—but they will be altered, never fear.

Omnes. How? How?

C. Wal. Do you see this hour-glass?—Here's the state—this air stands for the idlers;—this sand for the workers. When all the sand has run to the bottom, God in heaven just turns the hour-glass, and then—

C. Hugo. The world's upside down.

C. Wal. And the Lord have mercy upon us!

Omnes. On us! Do you call us the idlers?

C. Wal. Some dare to do so—But fear not—In the fulness of time, all that's lightest is sure to come to the the top again.

C. Hugo. But what rascal calls us idlers?

Omnes. Name, name.

C. Wal. Why, if you ask me—I heard a shrewd sermon the other day on that same idleness and immorality text of the Abbot's.—'Twas Conrad, the Princess's director, preached it. And a fashionable cap it is, though it will fit more than will like to wear it. Shall I give it you? Shall I preach?

C. Hugo. A tub for Varila! Stand on the table, now, toss back thy hood like any Franciscan, and preach away.

C. Wal. Idleness, quoth he, (Conrad, mind you,)—idleness and immorality! Where have they learnt them, but from you nobles? There was a saucy monk, for you. But there's worse coming. Religion? said he, how can they respect it, when they see you, 'their betters,' fattening on church lands, neglecting sacraments, defying excommunications, trading in benefices, hiring the clergy for your puppets and flatterers, making the ministry, the episcopate itself, a lumber-room wherein to stow away the idiots and spendthrifts of your families, the confidants of your mistresses, the cast-off pedagogues of your boys?

Omnes. The scoundrel!

C. Wal. Was he not?—But hear again—Immorality? roars he; and who has corrupted them but you? Have not you made every castle a weed-bed, from which the newest corruptions of the Court stick like thistle-down, about the empty heads of stable-boys and serving-maids? Have you not kept the poor worse housed than your dogs and your horses, worse fed than your pigs and your sheep? Is there an ancient house among you, again, of which village gossips do not whisper some dark story of lust and oppression, of decrepit debauchery, of hereditary doom?

Omnes. We'll hang this monk.

C. Wal. Hear me out, and you'll burn him. His sermon was like a hail-storm, the tail of the shower the sharpest. Idleness? he asked next of us all: How will they work, when they see you landlords sitting idle above them, in a fool's paradise of luxury and riot, never looking down but to squeeze from them an extra drop of honey—like sheep-boys stuffing themselves with blackberries while the sheep are licking up flukes in every ditch? And now you wish to leave the poor man in the slough, whither your neglect and your example have betrayed him, and made his too apt scholarship the excuse for your own remorseless greed? As a Christian, I am ashamed of you all: as a Churchman, doubly ashamed of those prelates, hired stalking-horses of the rich, who would fain gloss over their own sloth and cowardice with the wisdom which cometh not from above, but is earthly, sensual, devilish; aping the heartless cant of an aristocracy who made them—use them—and despise them. That was his sermon.

Abbot. Paul and Barnabas! What an outpouring of the spirit!—Were not his hoodship the Pope's legate, now—accidents might happen to him, going home at night; eh? Sir Hugo?

C. H. If he would but come my way!

For "the mule it was slow, and the lane it was dark,
When out of the copse leapt a gallant young spark,
Says, ''Tis not for nought you've been begging all
day:
So remember your toll, since you travel our way.'"

Abbot. Hush! Here comes the Landgrave.

LEWIS *enters.*

Lew. Good morrow, gentles. Why so warm, Count
Walter?
Your blessing, Father Abbot: what deep matters
Have called our worships to this conference?

C. H. [*Aside.*] Up, Count; you are spokesman.

3d Count. Most exalted Prince,
Whose peerless knighthood, like the remeant sun,
After too long a night, regilds our clay,

Late silvered by the reflex lunar beams
Of your celestial lady's matron graces—

Abbot. [*Aside.*] Ut vinum optimum amati mei
Dulciter descendens!

3d Count. Think not we mean to praise or disapprove—
The acts of saintly souls must only plead
In foro conscientiæ: grosser minds,
Whose humbler aim is but the public weal,
Know of no mesh which holds them: yet, great prince,
Some dare not see their sovereign's strength postponed
To private grace, and sigh, that generous hearts,
And ladies' tenderness, too oft forgetting
That wisdom is the highest charity,
Will interfere, in pardonable haste,
With heaven's stern providence.

Lew. We see your drift.
Go, sirrah, [*To a* PAGE,] pray the Princess to illumine
Our conclave with her beauties. 'Tis our manner
To hear no cause, of gentle or of simple,
Unless the accused and the accuser both
Meet face to face.

3d Count. Excuse, high-mightiness,—
We bring no accusation; facts, your Highness,
Wait for your sentence, not our præjudicium.

Lew. Give us the facts, then, sir; in the lady's presence,
Her nearness to ourselves—perchance her reasons—
May make them somewhat dazzling.

Abb. Nay, my Lord;
I, as a Churchman, though with these your nobles
Both in commission and opinion one,
Am yet most loth, my lord, to set my seal
To aught which this harsh world might call complaint
Against a princely saint—a chosen vessel—
An argosy celestial—in whom error
Is but the young luxuriance of her grace.
The Count of Varila, as bound to neither,
For both shall speak, and all which late has passed
Upon the matter of this famine open.

C. Wal. Why, if I must speak out—then I'll confess
To have stood by, and seen the Landgravine
Do most strange deeds; and in her generation
Show no more wit than other babes of light.
First, she has given away, to starving rascals,
The stores of grain, she might have sold, good lack!
For any price she asked; has pawned your jewels,
And mortgaged sundry farms, and all for food.
Has sunk vast sums in fever-hospitals,
For rogues whom famine sickened—almshouses
For sluts whose husbands died—schools for their brats.
Most sad vagaries! but there's worse to come.
The dulness of the Court has ruined trade:
The jewellers and clothiers don't come near us
The sempstresses, my lord, and pastry-cooks
Have quite forgot their craft; she has turned all heads,
And made the ladies starve, and wear old clothes,
And run about with her to nurse the sick,

Instead of putting gold in circulation
By balls, sham-fights, and dinners; 'tis most sad, sir,
But she has swept your treasury out as clean—
As was the widow's cruse, who fed Elijah.

Lew. Ruined, no doubt! Lo! here the culprit comes.

[ELIZABETH *enters.*

Come hither, dearest. These, my knights and nobles,
Lament your late unthrift; (your conscience speaks
The causes of their blame;) and wish you warned,
As wisdom is the highest charity,
No more to interfere, from private feeling
With heaven's stern laws, or maim the sovereign's wealth,
To save superfluous villains' worthless lives.

Eliz. Lewis!

Lew. Not I, fair, but my counsellors,
In courtesy, need some reply.

Eliz. My Lords;
Doubtless, you speak but as your duty bids you:
I know you love my husband; do you think
My love is less than yours? 'Twas for his honor
I dared not lose a single silly sheep
Of all the flock which God had trusted to him.
True, I had hoped by this—No matter what—
Since to your sense it bears a different hue.
I keep no logic. For my gifts, thank God,
They cannot be recalled; for those poor souls,
My pensioners—even for my husband's knightly name,
Oh! ask not back that slender loan of comfort
My folly has procured them: if, my Lords,

My public censure, or disgraceful penance
May expiate, and yet confirm my waste,
I offer this poor body to the buffets
Of sternest justice: where I dared not spare
My husband's lands, I dare not spare myself.

Lew. No! no! My noble sister? What? my Lords
If her love move you not, her wisdom may.
She knows a deeper statecraft, Sirs, than you;
She will not throw away the substance, Abbot,
To save the accident; waste living souls
To keep, or hope to keep, the means of life.
Our wisdom and our swords may fill our coffers,
But will they breed us men, my Lords, or mothers?
God blesses in the camp a noble rashness:
Then why not in the store-house? He that lends
To Him, need never fear to lose his venture.
Spend on, my Queen. You will not sell my castles?
Nay, you must leave us Neuburg, love, and Wartburg.
Their worn old old stones will hardly pay the carriage,
And foreign foes may pay untimely visits.

C. Wal. And home foes, too: if these philosophers
Put up the curb, my Lord, a half-link tighter,
The scythes will be among our horses' legs
Before next harvest.

Lew. Fear not for our welfare:
We have a guardian here, well skilled to keep
Peace for our seneschal, while angels, stooping
To catch the tears she sheds for us in absence,
Will sain us from the roaming adversary

With scents of Paradise. Farewell, my Lords.

Eliz. Nay,—I must pray your knighthoods—You must honor
Our dais and bower as private guests to-day.
Thanks for your gentle warning; may my weakness
To such a sin be never tempted more!

[*Exeunt* ELIZABETH *and* LEWIS.

C. Wal. Thus, as if virtue were not its own reward, is it paid over and above with beef and ale? Weep not tender-hearted Count! Though "generous hearts," my Lord, "and ladies' tenderness, too oft forget"—Truly spoken! Lord Abbot, does not your spiritual eye discern coals of fire on Count Hugo's head?

C. Hugo. Where, and a plague? Where?

C. Wal. Nay, I spake mystically,—there is nought there but what beer will quench before nightfall. Here, peeping rabbit, [*To a page at the door,*] out of your burrow, and show these gentles to their lodgings. We will meet at the gratias.

[*They go out.*

C. Wal. [*Alone.*] Well:—if Hugo is a brute, he at least makes no secret of it. He is an old boar, and honest; he wears his tushes outside, for a warning to all men. But for the rest!—Whited sepulchres! and not one of them but has half persuaded himself of his own benevolence. Of all cruelties, save me from your small pedant, — your closet philosopher, who has just courage enough to bestride his theory, without wit to see whither it will carry him. In experience — a child: in obstinacy a woman: in nothing a man, but in logic-chopping: instead of God's grace, a few schoolboy saws about benevolence, and industry, and independence—there is his metal. If the world will be mended on his principles, well. If not, poor world!—but principles must be carried out, though through blood and famine: for truly, man was made for theories, not theories for man. A doctrine is these men's God—touch but that shrine, and lo! your simpering philanthropist becomes as ruthless as a Dominican. [*Exit.*

SCENE IX.

ELIZABETH'S *Bower.* ELIZABETH *and* LEWIS *sitting together.*

SONG.

Eliz. Oh! that we two were Maying
Down the stream of the soft spring breeze;
Like children with violets playing
In the shade of the whispering trees.

Oh! that we two sat dreaming
On the sward of some sheep-trimmed down,
Watching the white mist steaming
Over river and mead and town.

Oh! that we two lay sleeping
In our nest in the churchyard sod,
With our limbs at rest on the quiet earth's breast,
And our souls at home with God!

Lew. Ah, turn away those swarthy diamonds' blaze!
Mine eyes are dizzy, and my faint sense reels
In the rich fragrance of those purple tresses.

Oh, to be thus, and thus, day after day!
To sleep, and wake, and find it yet no dream—
My atmosphere, my hourly food, such bliss
As to have dreamt of, five short years agone,
Had seemed a mad conceit.

Eliz. Five years agone?

Lew. I know not; for upon our marriage-day
I slipped from time into eternity;
Where each day teems with centuries of life,
And centuries were but one wedding morn.

Eliz. Lewis, I am too happy! floating higher
Than e'er my will had dared to soar, though able;
But circumstance, which is the will of God,
Beguiled my cowardice to that, which, darling,
I found most natural, when I feared it most.
Love would have had no strangeness in mine eyes,
Save from the prejudice which others taught me—
They should know best. Yet now this wedlock seems
A second infancy's baptismal robe,
A heaven, my spirit's antenatal home,
Lost in blind pining girlhood—found now, found!
[*Aside.*] What have I said? Do I blaspheme? Alas!
I neither made these thoughts, nor can unmake them.

Lew. Ay, marriage is the life-long miracle,
The self-begetting wonder, daily fresh;
The Eden, where the spirit and the flesh
Are one again, and new-born souls walk free,
And name in mystic language all things new,
Naked, and not ashamed. [ELIZ. *hides her face.*

Eliz. Oh! God! were that true!
[*Clasps him round the neck.*
There, there, no more—
I love thee, and I love thee, and I love thee—
More than rich thoughts can dream, or mad lips speak;
But how, or why, whether with soul or body,
I will not know. Thou art mine.—Why question further?
[*Aside.*] Ay, if I fall by loving, I will love,
And be degraded!—how? by my own troth plight?
No, but by thinking that I fall.—'Tis written
That whatsoe'er is not of faith is sin.—
Oh! Jesu Lord! Hast Thou not made me thus?
Mercy! My brain will burst: I cannot leave him!
Lew. Beloved, if I went away to war—
Eliz. Oh, God! More wars? More partings?
Lew. Nay, my sister—
My trust but longs to glory in its surety:
What would'st thou do?
Eliz. What I have done already.
Have I not followed thee, through drought and frost,
Through flooded swamps, rough glens, and wasted lands,
Even while I panted most with thy dear loan
Of double life?
Lew. My saint! but what if I bid thee
To be my seneschal, and here with prayers,
With sober thrift, and noble bounty shine,
Alone and peerless? And suppose—nay, start not—
I only said suppose—the war was long,
Our camps far off, and that some winter, love,

Or two, pent back this Eden stream, where now
Joys upon joys like sunlit ripples pass,
Alike, yet ever new.—What would'st thou do, love?

Eliz. A year? A year! A cold, blank, widowed year!
Strange, that mere words should chill my heart with fear—
This is no hall of doom—
No impious Soldan's feast of old,
Where o'er the madness of the foaming gold,
A fleshless hand its woe on tainted walls enrolled.
Yet by thy wild words raised,
In Love's most careless revel,
Looms through the future's fog a shade of evil,
And all my heart is glazed.—
Alas! What would I do?
I would lie down and weep, and weep,
Till the salt current of my tears should sweep
My soul, like floating weed, adown a fitful sleep,
A lingering half-night through.
Then when the mocking bells did wake
My hollow eyes to twilight gray,
I would address my spiritless limbs to pray,
And nerve myself with stripes to meet the weary day
And labour for thy sake.
Until by vigils, fasts and tears,
The flesh was grown so spare and light,
That I could slip its mesh, and flit by night
O'er sleeping sea and land to thee—or Christ—till morning light.

Peace! Why these fears?
Life is too short for mean anxieties:
Soul! thou must work, though blindfold.
Come, beloved,
I must turn robber.—I have begged of late
So oft, I fear to ask.—Give me thy purse.

Lew. No, not my purse:—stay—Where is all that gold
I gave you, when the Jews came here from Köln?

Eliz. Oh, those few coins? I spent them all next day
On a new chapel on the Eisenthal;
There were no choristers but nightingales—
No teachers there save bees: how long is this?
Have you turned niggard?

Lew. Nay; go ask my steward—
Take what you will—this purse I want myself.

Eliz. Ah! now I guess. You have some trinket for me—
You promised late to buy no more such baubles—
And now you are ashamed.—Nay, I must see—

[*Snatches his purse.* LEWIS *hides his face.*

Ah, God! what 's here? A new crusader's cross?
Whose? Nay, nay—turn not from me;—I guess all—
You need not tell me: it is very well—
According to the meed of my deserts:
Yes—very well.

Lew. Ah! love—look not so calm—

Eliz. Fear not—I shall weep soon.
How long is it since you vowed?

Lew. A week or more.

Eliz. Brave heart! And all that time your tenderness
Kept silence, knowing my weak foolish soul. [*Weeps.*
Oh, love! Oh, life! Late found, and soon, soon lost!
A bleak sunrise,—a treacherous morning gleam,—
And now, ere mid-day, all my sky is black
With whirling drifts once more! The march is fixed
For this day month, is 't not?

Lew. Alas, too true!

Eliz. O break not, heart! [CONRAD *enters.*
Ah! here my master comes,
No weeping before him.

Lew. Speak to the holy man:
He can give strength and comfort, which poor I
Need even more than you. Here, saintly master,
I leave her to your holy eloquence. Farewell!
God help us both! [*Exit* LEWIS.

Eliz. (*Rising.*) You know, Sir, that my husband has taken the cross?

Con. I do; all praise to God!

Eliz. But none to you:
Hard-hearted! Am I not enough your slave?
Can I obey you more when he is gone
Than now I do? Wherein, pray, has he hindered
This holiness of mine, for which you make me
Old ere my womanhood! [CONRAD *offers to go.*
Stay, Sir, and tell me
Is this the out-come of your "father's care?"

Was it not enough to poison all my joys
With foulest scruples ?—show me nameless sins,
Where I, unconscious babe, blessed God for all things,
But you must thus intrigue away my night
And plunge me down this gulf of widowhood!
And I not twenty yet—a girl—an orphan—
That cannot stand alone! Was I too happy?
Oh, God! what lawful bliss do I not buy
And balance with the smart of some sharp penance?
Hast thou no pity? None? Thou drivest me
To fiendish doubts: Thou, Jesus' messenger!

Con. This to your master!

Eliz. This to any one
Who dares to part me from my love.

Con. 'Tis well—
In pity to your weakness I must deign
To do what ne'er I did—excuse myself.
I say, I knew not of your husband's purpose;
God's spirit, not I, moved him: perhaps I sinned
In that I did not urge it myself.

Eliz. Thou traitor!
So thou would'st part us?

Con. Aught that makes thee greater
I'll dare, this very outburst proves in thee
Passions unsanctified, and carnal leanings
Upon the creatures thou would'st fain transcend.
Thou badest me cure thy weakness. Lo, God brings thee
The tonic cup I feared to mix:—be brave—

Drink it to the lees, and thou shalt find within
A pearl of price.

Eliz. 'Tis bitter!

Con. Bitter, truly:
Even I, to whom the storm of earthly love
Is but a dim remembrance—Courage! Courage!
There 's glory in 't; fulfil thy sacrifice;
Give up thy noblest on the noblest service
God's sun has looked on, since the chosen twelve
Went conquering, and to conquer, forth. If he fall—

Eliz. Oh, spare mine ears!

Con. He falls a blessed martyr,
To bid thee welcome through the gates of pearl;
And next to his shall thine own guerdon be
If thou devote him willing to thy God.
Wilt thou?

Eliz. Have mercy!

Con. Wilt thou? Sit not thus
Watching the sightless air: no angel in it
But asks thee what I ask: the fiend alone
Delays thy coward flesh. Wilt thou devote him?

Eliz. I will devote him;—a crusader's wife!
I'll glory in it. Thou speakest words from God—
And God shall have him! Go now—good, my master;
My poor brain swims. [*Exit* CONRAD.
Yes—a crusader's wife!
And a crusader's widow!

[*Bursts into tears, and dashes herself on the floor.*]

SCENE X.

A Street in the Town of Schmalcald. Bodies of Crusading Troops defiling past. LEWIS *and* ELIZABETH *with their Suite in the foreground.*

Lew. Alas! the time is near; I must be gone—
There are our liegemen; how you'll welcome us,
Returned in triumph, bowed with paynim spoils,
Beneath the victor cross, to part no more!
Eliz. Yes—we shall part no more, where next we meet.
Enough to have stood here once on such an errand!
Lew. The bugle calls.—Farewell, my love, my lady,
Queen, sister, saint! One last long kiss.—Farewell!
Eliz. One kiss—and then another—and another—
Till 'tis too late to go—and so return—
Oh God! forgive that craven thought! There, take him
Since Thou dost need him. I have kept him ever
Thine, when most mine; and shall I now deny Thee?
Oh! go—yes, go—Thou 'lt not forget to pray,
[LEWIS *goes.*
With me, at our old hour? Alas! he 's gone
And lost—thank God he hears me not—forever.
Why look'st thou so, poor girl? I say, forever.
The day I found the bitter blessed cross,
Something did strike my heart like keen cold steel,
Which quarries daily there with dead dull pains—
Whereby I know that we shall meet no more.
Come! Home, maids, home! Prepare me widow's weeds—
For he is dead to me, and I must soon

Die too to him, and many things; and mark me—
Breathe not his name, lest this love-pampered heart
Should sicken to vain yearnings—Lost! lost! lost!

Lady. Oh stay, and watch this pomp.

Eliz. Well said—we 'll stay; so this bright enterprise
Shall blanch our private clouds, and steep our soul
Drunk with the spirit of great christendom.

CRUSADER CHORUS.

[*Men at Arms pass singing.*]

The tomb of God before us,
Our fatherland behind,
Our ships shall leap o'er billows steep,
Before a charmed wind.

Above our van great angels
Shall fight along the sky;
While martyrs pure and crowned saints,
To God for rescue cry.

The red-cross knights and yeomen
Throughout the holy town,
In faith and might, on left and right,
Shall tread the paynim down.

Till on the Mount Moriah
The Pope of Rome shall stand;
The Kaiser and the King of France
Shall guard him on each hand.

There shall he rule all nations,
With crozier and with sword;
And pour on all the heathen,
The wrath of Christ the Lord.

[*Women—bystanders.*]

Christ is a rock in the bare salt land,
To shelter our knights from the sun and sand;
Christ the Lord is a summer sun,
To ripen the grain while they are gone.

Then you who fight in the bare salt land,
And you who work at home,
Fight and work for Christ the Lord,
Until His kingdom come.

[*Old Knights pass.*]

Our stormy sun is sinking;
Our sands are running low;
In one fair fight, before the night,
Our hard-worn hearts shall glow.

We cannot pine in cloister;
We cannot fast and pray;
The sword which built our load of guilt,
Must wipe that guilt away.

We know the doom before us;
The dangers of the road;

Have mercy, mercy, Jesu blest,
When we lie low in blood.

When we lie gashed and gory,
The holy walls within,
Sweet Jesu, think upon our end,
And wipe away our sin.

[*Boy Crusaders pass.*]

The Christ-child sits on high;
He looks through the merry blue sky;
He holds in His hand a bright lily-band,
For the boys who for Him die.

On holy Mary's arm,
Wrapt safe from terror and harm,
Lulled by the breeze in the paradise trees,
Their souls sleep soft and warm.

Knight David, young and true,
The giant Soldan slew,
And our arms so light, for the Christ-child's
right,
Like noble deeds can do.

[*Young Knights pass.*]

The rich East blooms fragrant before us;
All Fairy-land beckons us forth;
We must follow the crane in her flight o'er the main,
From the posts and the moors of the North.

Our sires in the youth of the nations
Swept westward through plunder and blood,
But a holier quest calls us back to the East,
We fight for the kingdom of God.

Then shrink not, and sigh not, fair ladies,
The red cross which flames on each arm and each shield,
Through philtre and spell, and the black charms of hell,
Shall shelter our true love in camp and in field.

[*Old Monk looking after them.*]

Jerusalem, Jerusalem!
The burying-place of God!
Why gay and bold, in steel and gold,
O'er the paths where Christ hath trod?

[*The Scene closes.*

ACT III.

Scene I.

A Chamber in the Wartburg. Elizabeth *sitting in Widow's weeds;* Guta *and* Isentrudis *by her.*

Isen. What? Always thus, my princess? Is this wise,
By day with fasts, and ceaseless coil of labour;
About the ungracious poor—hands, eyes, feet, brain,
O'ertasked alike—'mid sin and filth, which make
Each sense a plague—by night with cruel stripes,
And weary watchings on the freezing stone,
To double all your griefs, and burn life's candle,
As village gossips say, at either end?
The good book bids the heavy-hearted drink,
And so forget their woe.

Eliz. 'Tis written too
In that same book, nurse, that the days shall come,
When the bridegroom shall be taken away—and then—
Then shall they mourn and fast: I needed weaning
From sense and earthly joys; by this way only
May I win God to leave in mine own hands
My luxury's cure: oh! I may bring him back,
By working out to its full depth the chastening
The need of which his loss proves: I but barter
Less grief for greater—pain for widowhood.

Isen. And death for life—your cheeks are wan and sharp

As any three-days' moon—you are shifting always
Uneasily and stiff, now, on your seat,
As from some secret pain.

Eliz. Why watch me thus?
You cannot know—and yet you know too much—
I tell you, nurse, pain 's comfort, when the flesh
Aches with the aching soul in harmony,
And even in woe, we are one: the heart must speak
Its passion's strangeness in strange symbols out,
Or boil, till it bursts inly.

Guta. Yet, methinks,
You might have made this widowed solitude
A holy rest—a spell of soft gray weather,
Beneath whose fragrant dews all tender thoughts
Might bud and burgeon.

Eliz. That 's a gentle dream;
But nature shows nought like it: every winter,
When the great sun has turned his face away,
The earth goes down into the vale of grief,
And fasts, and weeps, and shrouds herself in sables,
Leaving her wedding-garlands to decay—
Then leaps in spring to his returning kisses—
As I may yet!—

Isen. There, now—my foolish child!
You faint: come—come to your chamber—

Eliz. Oh, forgive me!
But hope at times throngs in so rich and full,
It mads the brain like wine: come with me, nurse,
Sit by me, lull me calm with gentle tales

Of noble ladies wandering in the wild wood,
Fed on chance earth-nuts, and wild strawberries,
Or milk of silly sheep, and woodland doe.
Or how fair Magdalen 'mid desert sands
Wore out in prayer her lonely blissful years,
Watched by bright angels, till her modest tresses
Wove to her pearled feet their golden shroud.
Come, open all your lore.

[SOPHIA *and* AGNES *enter.*]

My mother-in-law!
[*Aside.*] Shame on thee, heart! why sink, whene'er we meet?

Soph. Daughter, we know of old thy strength, of metal
Beyond us worldlings: shrink not, if the time
Be come which needs its use—

Eliz. What means this preface? Ah! your looks are big
With sudden woes—speak out.

Soph. Be calm, and hear
The will of God toward my son, thy husband.

Eliz. What? is he captive? Why then—what of that?
There are friends will rescue him—there's gold for ransom—
We'll sell all our castles—live in bowers of rushes—
Oh God! that I were with him in the dungeon!

Soph. He is not taken.

Eliz. No! he would have fought to the death!

There 's treachery! What paynim dog dare face
His lance, who naked braved yon lion's rage,
And eyed the cowering monster to his den?
Speak! Has he fled? or worse?

Soph. Child, he is dead.

Eliz. [*Clasping her hands on her knees.*] The world is dead to me, and all its smiles!

Isen. Oh, woe! my prince! and doubly woe, my daughter!

[ELIZABETH *springs up and rushes out.*

Oh, stop her—stop my child! She will go mad—
Dash herself down—Fly—Fly—She is not made
Of hard, light stuff, like you.

[ISENTRUDIS *and* GUTA *run out.*

Soph. I had expected some such passionate outbreak
At the first news: you see now, Lady Agnes,
These saints, who fain would 'wean themselves from earth,'
Still yield to the affections they despise
When the game 's earnest—Now—ere they return—
Your brother, child, is dead——

Agnes. I know it too well.
So young—so brave—so blest!—And she—she loved him—
Oh! I repent of all the foolish scoffs
With which I crossed her.

Soph. Yes—the Landgrave 's dead—
Attend to me—Alas! my son! my son!
He was my first-born! But he has a brother—

Agnes! we must not let this foreign gipsy,
Who, as you see, is scarce her own wits' mistress,
Flaunt sovereign over us, and our broad lands,
To my son's prejudice—There are barons, child,
Who will obey a knight, but not a saint:
I must at once to them.

Agnes. Oh, let me stay!

Soph. As you shall please—Your brother's landgravate
Is somewhat to you, surely—and your smiles
Are worth gold pieces in a court intrigue.
For her, on her own principles, a downfall
Is a chastening mercy—and a likely one.

Agnes. Oh! let me stay, and comfort her!

Soph. Romance!
You girls adore a scene—as lookers on.

[*Exit* SOPHIA.

Agnes. [*Alone.*] Well spoke the old monks, peaceful watching life's turmoil,
"Eyes which look heaven-ward, weeping still we see:
God's love with keen flame purges, like the lightning flash,
Gold which is purest, purer still must be."

[GUTA *enters.*]

Alas! Returned alone! Where has my sister been?

Guta. Thank heaven, you hear alone, for such sad sight would haunt
Henceforth your young hopes—crush your shuddering fancy down

With dread of like fierce anguish.

Agnes. Speak! Oh, speak!

Guta. You saw her bound forth: we towards her bower in haste
Ran trembling: spell-bound there, before her bridal-bed
She stood, while wan smiles flickered, like the northern dawn,
Across her worn cheek's ice-field; keenest memories then
Rushed with strong shudderings through her—as the winged shaft
Springs from the tense nerve, so her passion hurled her forth,
Sweeping, like fierce ghost, on through hall and corridor,
Tearless, with wide eyes staring, while a ghastly wind
Moaned on through roof and rafter, and the empty helms
Along the walls rang clattering, and above her waved
Dead heroes' banners: swift and yet more swift she drove
Still seeking aimless; sheer against the opposing wall
At last dashed reckless—there with frantic fingers clutched
Blindly the ribbed oak, till that frost of rage
Dissolved itself in tears, and like a babe,
With inarticulate moans, and folded hands,
She followed those who led her, as if the sun
On her life's dial had gone back seven years,
And she were once again the dumb sad child
We knew her ere she married.

Isen. [*entering.*] As after wolf wolf presses, leaping through the snow-glades,
So woe on woe throngs surging up.

Guta. What? treason?

Isen. Treason, and of the foulest. From her state she's rudely thrust;
Her keys are seized; her weeping babies pent from her:
The wenches stop their sobs to sneer askance,
And greet their fallen censor's new mischance.

Agnes. Alas! Who dared to do this wrong?

Isen. Your mother and your mother's son—
Judge you, if it was knightly done.

Guta. See! see! she comes, with heaving breast,
With bursting eyes, and purple brow:
Oh, that the traitors saw her now!
They know not, sightless fools, the heart they break.

[ELIZABETH *enters slowly.*]

Eliz. He is in purgatory now! Alas!
Angels! be pitiful! deal gently with him!
His sins were gentle! That's one cause left for living—
To pray, and pray for him: why all these months—
I prayed,—and here's my answer: Dead of a fever!
Why thus? so soon! Only six years for love!
While any formal, heartless matrimony,
Patched up by Court intrigues, and threats of cloisters,
Drags on for six times six, and peasant slaves
Grow old on the same straw, and hand in hand
Slip from life's oozy bank, to float at ease.

[*A knocking at the door.*

That 's some petitioner.
Go to—I will not hear them: why should I work,
When he is dead? Alas! was that my sin?
Was he, not Christ, my lode-star? Why not warn me?
Too late! What 's this foul dream? Dead at Otranto—
Parched by Italian suns—no woman by him—
He was too chaste! Nought but rude men to nurse!—
If I had been there, I should have watched by him—
Guessed every fancy—God! I might have saved him!

[*A servant-man bursts in.*

Servant. Madam, the Landgrave gave me strict commands—

Isen. The Landgrave, dolt?

Eliz. I might have saved him!

Servant. [*to Isen.*] Ay, saucy madam!—
The Landgrave Henry, lord and master,
Freer than the last, and yet no waster,
Who will not stint a poor knave's beer,
Or spin out Lent through half the year.
Why—I see double!

Eliz. Who spoke there of the Landgrave? What 's this drunkard?
Give him his answer—'Tis no time for mumming—

Serv. The Landgrave Henry bade me see you out
Safe through his gates, and that at once, my Lady.
Come!

Eliz. Why—that 's hasty—I must take my children—
Ah! I forgot—they would not let me see them.
I must pack up my jewels—

Serv. You 'll not need it—
His Lordship has the keys.

Eliz. He has indeed.
Why, man!—I am thy children's godmother—
I nursed thy wife myself in the black sickness—
Art thou a bird, that when the old tree falls,
Flits off, and sings in the sapling?

[*The man seizes her arm.*

Keep thine hands off—
I'll not be shamed—Lead on. Farewell, my Ladies.
Follow not! There 's want to spare on earth already;
And mine own woe is weight enough for me.
Go back, and say, Elizabeth has yet
Eternal homes, built deep in poor men's hearts;
And, in the alleys underneath the wall,
Has bought with sinful mammon heavenly treasure,
More sure than adamant, purer than white whales' bone,
Which now she claims. Lead on: a people's love shall
right me. [*Exit with servant.*

Guta. Where now, dame?

Isen. Where, but after her?

Guta. True heart!
I'll follow to the death. [*Exeunt.*

SCENE II.

A Street. ELIZABETH *and* GUTA *at the door of a Convent. Monks in the Porch.*

Eliz. You are afraid to shelter me—afraid.
And so you thrust me forth, to starve and freeze.

Soon said. Why palter o'er these mean excuses,
Which tempt me to despise you?
Monks. Ah! my lady,
We know your kindness—but we poor religious—
Are bound to obey God's ordinance, and submit
Unto the powers that be, who have forbidden
All men, alas! to give you food or shelter.
Eliz. Silence! I'll go. Better in God's hand than man's,
He shall kill us, if we die. This bitter blast
Warping the leafless willows, yon white snow-storms,
Whose wings, like vengeful angels, cope the vault,
They are God's,—We 'll trust to them. [*Monks go in.*
Guta. Mean-spirited!
Fair frocks hide foul hearts. Why their altar now
Is blazing with your gifts.
Eliz. How long their altar?
To God I gave—and God shall pay me back.
Fool! to have put my trust in living man,
And fancied that I bought God's love, by buying
The greedy thanks of these His earthly tools!
Well—here 's one lesson learnt! I thank thee, Lord!
Henceforth I'll straight to Thee, and to Thy poor.
What? Isentrudis not returned? Alas!
Where are those children?
They will not have the heart to keep them from me—
Oh! have the traitors harmed them?
Guta. Do not think it.
The dowager has a woman's heart.

Eliz. Ay, ay—
But she 's a mother—and mothers will dare all things—
Oh! Love can make us fiends, as well as angels.
My babies! Weeping? Oh have mercy, Lord!
On me heap all thy wrath—I understand it:
What can blind senseless terror do for them?
Guta. Plead, plead your penances! Great God, consider
All she has done and suffered, and forbear
To smite her like a worldling?
Eliz. Silence, girl!
I'd plead my deeds, if mine own character,
My strength of will had fathered them: but no—
They are His, who worked them in me, in despite
Of mine own selfish and luxurious will—
Shall I bribe Him with His own? For pain, I tell thee
I need more pain than mine own will inflicts,
Pain which shall break that will.—Yet spare them, Lord!
Go to—I am a fool to wish them life—
And greater fool to miscall life, this headache—
This nightmare of our gross and crude digestion—
This fog which steams up from our freezing clay—
While waking heaven 's beyond. No! slay them, traitors!
Cut through the channels of those innocent breaths
Whose music charmed my lone nights, ere they learn
To love the world, and hate the wretch who bore them!
[*Weeps.*

Guta. This storm will blind us both: come here, and shield you
Behind this buttress.
Eliz. What's a wind to me?
I can see up the street here, if they come—
They do not come!—Oh! my poor weanling lambs—
Struck dead by carrion ravens!
What then, I have borne worse. But yesterday
I thought I had a husband—and now—now!
Guta! He called a holy man before he died?
Guta. The Bishop of Jerusalem, 'tis said,
With holy oil, and with the blessed body
Of Him for whom he died, did speed him duly
Upon his heavenward flight.
Eliz. Oh happy bishop!
Where are those children? If I had but seen him:
I could have borne all then. One word—one kiss!
Hark! What's that rushing! White doves—one—two—three—
Fleeing before the gale.—My children's spirits!
Stay, babies—stay for me! What! Not a moment?
And I so nearly ready to be gone?
Guta. Still on your children?
Eliz. Oh! this grief is light
And floats a-top—well, well; it hides awhile
That gulf too black for speech—My husband's dead!
I dare not think on 't.
A small bird dead in the snow! Alas! poor minstrel!
A week ago, before this very window,

He warbled, may be, to the slanting sunlight;
And housewives blest him for a merry singer:
And now he freezes at their doors, like me.
Poor foolish brother! didst thou look for payment?

Guta. But thou hast light in darkness—He has none—
The bird 's the sport of time, while our life's floor
Is laid upon eternity; no crack in it
But shows the underlying heaven.

Eliz. Art sure?
Does this look like it, girl! No—I'll trust yet—
Some have gone mad for less; but why should I?
Who live in time, and not eternity.
'Twill end, girl, end; no cloud across the sun
But passes at the last, and gives us back
The face of God once more.

Guta. See here they come,
Dame Isentrudis and your children, all
Safe down the cliff path, through the whirling snow-drifts.

Eliz. Oh Lord, my Lord! I thank Thee!
Loving, and merciful, and tender-hearted,
And even in fiercest wrath remembering mercy.
Lo! here 's my ancient foe. What want you, Sir?

[HUGO *enters.*

Hugo. Want? Faith, 'tis you who want, not I, my Lady—
I hear, you are gone a begging through the town;
So for your husband's sake, I'll take you in;
For though I can't forget your scurvy usage,

He was a very honest sort of fellow,
Though mad as a March hare; so come you in.

Eliz. But know you, sir, that all my husband's vassals
Are bidden bar their doors to me?

Hugo. I know it:
And therefore come you in: my house is mine:
No upstarts shall lay down the law to me;
Not they, mass: but mind you, no canting here—
No psalm-singing; all candles out at eight:
Beggars must not be choosers. Come along!

Eliz. I thank you, Sir; and for my children's sake
I do accept your bounty. [*Aside.*] Down, proud heart—
Bend lower—lower ever: thus God deals with thee.
Go, Guta, send the children after me. [*Exeunt severally.*

[*Two Peasants enter.*]

1st Peas. Here's Father January taken a lease of March month, and put in Jack Frost for bailiff. What be I to do for spring-feed if the weather holds,—and my ryelands as bare as the back of my hand?

2d Peas. That's your luck. Freeze on, say I, and may Mary Mother send us snow a yard deep. I have ten ton of hay yet to sell—ten ton, man—there's my luck: every man for himself, and—Why, here comes that handsome canting girl, used to be about the Princess.

[GUTA *enters.*]

Guta. Well met, fair sirs! I know you kind and loyal,
And bound by many a favor to my mistress:
Say, will you bear this letter for her sake

Unto her aunt, the rich and holy lady
Who rules the nuns of Kitzingen.

2d Peas. If I do, pickle me in a barrel among cabbage.
She told me once, God's curse would overtake me,
For grinding of the poor: her turn 's come now.

Guta. Will you, then, help her? She will pay you richly.

1st Peas. Ay? How dame? How? Where will the money come from?

Guta. God knows—

1st Peas. And you do not.

Guta. Why, but last winter,
When all your stacks were fired, she lent you gold.

1st Peas. Well—I'll be generous: as the times are hard,
Say, if I take your letter, will you promise
To marry me yourself?

Guta. Ay, marry you,
Or any thing, if you 'll but go to-day:
At once, mind. [*Giving him the Letter.*

1st Peas. Ay, I'll go. Now, you 'll remember?

Guta. Straight to her ladyship at Kitzengen.
God and his saints deal with you, as you deal
With us this day. [*Exit.*

2d Peas. What! art thou fallen in love promiscuously?

1st Peas. Why, see, now, man; she has her mistress' ear;
And if I marry her, no doubt they 'll make me
Bailiff, or land-steward; and there 's noble pickings
In that same line.

2d Peas. Thou hast bought a pig in a poke:
Her priest will shrive her off from such a bargain.

1st Peas. Dost think? Well—I'll not fret myself about it.
See, now, before I start, I must get home
Those pigs from off the forest; chop some furze;
And then to get my supper, and my horse's:
And then a man will need to sit awhile,
And take his snack of brandy for digestion;
And then to fettle up my sword and buckler;
And then, bid 'em all good bye: and by that time
'Twill be most nightfall—I'll just go to-morrow.
Off—here she comes again. [*Exeunt.*

[ISENTRUDIS *and* GUTA *enter, with the Children.*]

Guta. I warned you of it; I knew she would not stay
An hour, thus treated like a slave—an idiot.

Isen. Well, 'twas past bearing: so we are thrust forth
To starve again: Are all your jewels gone?

Guta. All pawned and eaten—and for her, you know,
She never bore the worth of one day's meal
About her dress, We can but die—No foe
Can ban us from that rest.

Isen. Ay, but these children!—Well—if it must be,
Here, Guta, pull off this old withered hand
My wedding-ring; the man who gave it me
Should be in heaven—and there he'll know my heart.
Take it, girl, take it. Where's the princess now?
She stopped before a crucifix to pray;
But why so long?

Guta. Oh! prayer, to her rapt soul,
Is like the drunkenness of the autumn bee,
Who scent-enchanted, on the latest flower,
Heedless of cold, will linger listless on,
And freeze in odorous dreams.

Isen. Ah! here she comes.

Guta. Dripping from head to foot with wet and mire!
How 's this?

[ELIZABETH *entering.*]

Eliz. How? Oh, my fortune rises to full flood:
I met a friend just now, who told me truths
Wholesome and stern, of my deceitful heart—
Would God I had known them earlier!—and enforced
Her lesson so, as I shall ne'er forget it
In body or in mind.

Isen. What means all this?

Eliz. You know the stepping-stones across the ford:
There as I passed, a certain aged crone,
Whom I had fed, and nursed, year after year,
Met me mid-stream—thrust past me stoutly on—
And rolled me headlong in the freezing mire.
There as I lay and weltered—"Take that, madam,
For all your selfish hypocritic pride
Which thought it such a vast humility
To wash us poor folks' feet, and use our bodies
For staves to build withal your Jacob's-ladder.
What! you would mount to heaven upon our backs?
The ass has thrown his rider?" She crept on—

I washed my garments in the brook hard by—
And came here, all the wiser.

Guta. Miscreant hag!

Isen. Alas, you 'll freeze.

Guta. Who could have dreamt the witch
Could harbor such a spite?

Eliz. Nay, who could dream
She would have guessed my heart so well? Dull boors
See deeper than we think, and hide within
Those leathern hulls unfathomable truths,
Which we amid thought's glittering mazes lose.
They grind among the iron facts of life,
And have no time for self-deception.

Isen. Come—
Put on my cloak—stand here, behind the wall.
Oh! is it come to this? She 'll die of cold.

Guta. Ungrateful fiend!

Eliz. Let be—we must not think on 't.
The scoff was true—I thank her—I thank God—
This too I needed. I had built myself
A Babel-tower, whose top should reach to heaven,
Of poor men's praise and prayers, and subtle pride
At mine own alms. 'Tis crumbled into dust!
Oh! I have leant upon an arm of flesh—
And here 's its strength! I'll walk by faith—by faith!
And rest my weary heart on Christ alone—
On Him, the all-sufficient!
Shame on me! dreaming thus about myself,
While you stand shivering here. [*To her little Son.*

Art cold, young knight?
Knights must not cry—Go slide, and warm thyself.
Where shall we lodge to-night?

Isen. There 's no place open,
But that foul tavern, where we lay last night.

Elizabeth's Son, [*clinging to her.*] Oh, mother, mother! go not to that house—
Among those fierce lank men, who laughed, and scowled,
And showed their knives, and sang strange ugly songs
Of you and us. Oh, mother! let us be!

Eliz. Hark! look! His father's voice!—his very eye—
Opening so slow and sad, then sinking down
In luscious rest again!

Isen. Bethink you, child—

Eliz. Oh yes—I'll think—we 'll to our tavern friends;
If they be brutes, 'twas my sin left them so.

Guta. 'Tis but for a night or two: three days will bring
The Abbess hither.

Isen. And then to Bamberg straight
For knights and men at arms! Your uncle's wrath—

Guta. [*Aside.*] Hush, hush! you 'll fret her, if you talk of vengeance.

Isen. Come to our shelter.

Children. Oh stay here, stay here!
Behind these walls.

Eliz. Ay—stay awhile in peace. The storms are still.
Beneath her eider robe the patient earth

Watches in silence for the sun: we 'll sit
And gaze up with her at the changeless heaven,
Until this tyranny be overpast.
Come [*Aside.*] Lost! Lost! Lost!
[*They enter a neighbouring Ruin.*]

SCENE III.

A Chamber in the Bishop's Palace at Bamberg.
ELIZABETH *and* GUTA.

Guta. You have determined?
Eliz. Yes—to go with him.
I have kept my oath too long to break it now.
I will to Marpurg, and there waste away
In meditation and in pious deeds,
Till God shall set me free.
Guta. How if your uncle
Will have you marry? Day and night, they say,
He talks of nothing else.
Eliz. Never, girl, never!
Save me from that at least, oh, God!
Guta. He spoke
Of giving us, your maidens, to his knights
In carnal wedlock: but I fear him not:
For God's own word is pledged to keep me pure—
I am a maid.
Eliz. And I, alas! am none!
Oh, Guta! dost thou mock my widowed love?
I was a wife—'tis true: I was not worthy—
But there was meaning in that first wild fancy;

'Twas but the innocent springing of the sap—
The witless yearning of an homeless heart—
Do I not know that God has pardoned me?
But now—to rouse and turn of mine own will,
In cool and full foreknowledge, this worn soul
Again to that, which, when God thrust it on me,
Bred but one shame of ever-gnawing doubt,
Were—No, my burning cheeks! We'll say no more.
Ah! loved and lost! Though God's chaste grace should fail me,
My weak idolatry of thee would give
Strength that should keep me true: with mine own hands
I'd mar this tear-worn face, till petulant man
Should loathe its scarred and shapeless ugliness.

Guta. But your poor children? What becomes of them?

Eliz. Oh! she who was not worthy of a husband
Does not deserve his children. What are they, darlings,
But snares to keep me from my heavenly spouse
By picturing the spouse I must forget?
Well—'tis blank horror. Yet if grief's good for me,
Let me go down into grief's blackest pit,
And follow out God's cure by mine own deed.

Guta. What will your kinsfolk think?

Eliz. What will they think?
What pleases them. That argument's a staff
Which breaks whene'er you lean on't. Trust me, girl,
That fear of man sucks out love's soaring ether,

Baffles faith's heavenward eyes, and drops us down,
To float, like plumeless birds, on any stream.
Have I not proved it?
There was a time with me, when every eye
Did scorch like flame: if one looked cold on me,
I strait accused myself of mortal sins:
Each fopling was my master: I have lied
From very fear of mine own serving-maids.
That 's past, thank God's good grace!

Guta. And now you leap
To the other end of the line.

Eliz. In self-defence—
I am too weak to live by half my conscience;
I have no wit to way and choose the mean;
Life is too short for logic; what I do
I must do simply; God alone must judge—
For God alone shall guide, and God's elect—
I shrink from earth's chill frosts too much to crawl—
I have snapped opinion's chains, and now I'll soar
Up to the blazing sunlight, and be free.

THE BISHOP OF BAMBERG *enters.* CONRAD *following.*

Bishop. The Devil plagued St. Antony in the likeness of a lean friar! Between mad monks and mad women, bedlam's broke loose, I think.

Con. When the spirit first descended on the elect, seculars then, too, said mocking, "These men are full of new wine."

Bishop. Seculars, truly! If I had not in my secularity

picked up a spice of chivalry to the ladies, I should long ago have turned out you and your regulars, to cant elsewhere. Plague on this gout—I must sit.

Eliz. Let me settle your cushion, uncle.

Bishop. So! girl! I sent for you from Botenstain. I had a mind, now, to have kept you there until your wits returned, and you would say Yes to some young noble suitor. As if I had not had trouble enough about your dower!—If I had had to fight for it, I should not have minded:—but these palavers and conferences have fretted me into the gout: and now you would throw all away again, tired with your toy, I suppose. What shall I say to the Counts, Varila, and the Cupbearer, and all the noble knights who will hazard their lands and lives, in trying to right you with that traitor? I am ashamed to look them in the face! To give all up to the villain! To pay him for his treason!

Eliz. Uncle, I give but what to me is worthless. He loves these baubles—let him keep them then: I have my dower.

Bishop. To squander on nuns and beggars, at this rogue's bidding? Why not marry some honest man? You may have your choice of kings and princes; and if you have been happy with one gentleman, Mass! say I, why can't you be happy with another? What saith the Scripture? "I will that the younger widows marry, bear children,"—not run after monks, and what not—What 's good for the filly, is good for the mare, say I.

Eliz. Uncle, I soar now at a higher pitch—
To be henceforth the bride of Christ alone.

Bishop. Ahem!—a pious notion—in moderation. We must be moderate, my child, moderate: I hate overdoing any thing—especially religion.

Con. Madam, between your uncle and myself
This question in your absence were best mooted.
[*Exit* ELIZABETH.

Bishop. How, priest? do you order her about like a servant-maid?

Con. The saints forbid! Now—ere I lose a moment— [*Kneeling.*
[*Aside.*] All things to all men be—and so save some—
[*Aloud.*] Forgive, your grace, forgive me,
If mine unmannered speech in aught have clashed
With your more tempered and melodious judgment:
Your courage will forgive an honest warmth.
God knows, I serve no private interests.

Bishop. Your orders, hey? to wit?

Con. My lord, my lord,
There may be higher aims: but what I said,
I said but for our Church, and our cloth's honor.
Ladies' religion, like their love, we know,
Requires a gloss of verbal exaltation,
Lest the sweet souls should understand themselves;
And clergymen must talk up to the mark.

Bishop. We all know, Gospel preached in the mother-tongue
Sounds too like common sense.

Con. Or too unlike it:
You know the world, your grace; you know the sex—

Bishop. Ahem! As a spectator.

Con. Philosophicè—
Just so—You know their rage for shaven crowns—
How they 'll deny their God—but not their priest—
Flirts—scandal-mongers—in default of both come
Platonic love—worship of art and genius—
Idols which make them dream of heaven, as girls
Dream of their sweethearts, when they sleep on bride-cake.
It saves from worse—we are not all Abelards.

Bishop. [*Aside.*] Some of us have his tongue, if not his face.

Con. There lies her fancy; do but balk her of it—
She 'll bolt to cloisters, like a rabbit scared.
Head her from that—she 'll wed some pink-faced boy—
The more low-bred and penniless, the likelier.
Send her to Marpurg, and her brain will cool.
Tug at the kite, 'twill only soar the higher:
Give it but line, my lord, 'twill drop like slate.
Use but that eagle's glance, whose daring foresight
In chapter, camp, and council wins the wonder
Of timid trucklers—Scan results and outcomes—
The scale is heavy in your grace's favour.

Bishop. Bah! priest! What can this Marpurg-madness do for me?

Con. Leave you the tutelage of all her children.

Bishop. Thank you—to play the drynurse to three starving brats.

Con. The minor's guardian guards the minors' lands.

Bishop. Unless they are pitched away in building hospitals.

Con. Instead of fattening in your wisdom's keeping.

Bishop. Well, well—but what gross scandal to the family!

Con. The family, my lord, would gain a saint.

Bishop. Ah! monk, that canonization costs a frightful sum.

Con. Those fees, just now, would gladly be remitted.

Bishop. These are the last days, faith, when Rome 's too rich to take!

Con. The Saints forbid, my lord, the fisher's see
Were so o'ercursed by Mammon! But you grieve,
I know, to see foul weeds of heresy
Of late o'errun your diocese.

Bishop. Ay, curse them!
I've hanged some dozens.

Con. Worthy of yourself!
But yet the faith needs here some mighty triumph—
Some bright example, whose resplendent blaze
May tempt that fluttering tribe within the pale
Of Holy Church again—

Bishop. To singe their wings?

Con. They 'll not come near enough. Again—there are
Who dare arraign your prowess, and assert
A churchman's energies were better spent
In pulpits, than the tented field. Now mark—
Mark, what a door is opened. Give but scope

To this her huge capacity for sainthood—
Set her, a burning and a shining light
To all your people.—Such a sacrifice,
Such loan to God of your own flesh and blood,
Will silence envious tongues, and prove you wise
For the next world as for this; will clear your name
From calumnies which argue worldliness;
Buy of itself the joys of paradise;
And clench your lordship's interest with the pontiff.

Bishop. Well, well, we'll think on't.

Con. Sir, I doubt you not.

[*Re-enter* ELIZABETH.] Uncle, I am determined.

Bishop. So am I.
You shall to Marpurg with this holy man.

Eliz. Ah, there you speak again like mine own uncle.
I'll go—to rest [*aside*] and die. I only wait
To see the bones of my beloved laid
In some fit resting-place. A messenger
Proclaims them near. Oh God!

Bishop. We'll go, my child,
And meeting them with all due honour, show
In our own worship, honourable minds.

[*Exit* ELIZABETH.

Bishop. A messenger! How far off are they, then?

Serv. Some two days' journey, sir.

Bishop. Two days' journey, and nought prepared? Here chaplain—Brother Hippodamas! Chaplain, I say! [HIPPODAMAS *enters.*] Call the apparitor—ride off with him, right and left.—Don't wait even to take your hawk—Tell my knights to be with me, with all their men-at-arms, at noon on the second day. Let all be of the best, say—the brightest of arms and the newest of garments. Mass! we must show our smartest before these crusaders—they 'll be full of new fashions, I warrant 'em—the monkeys that have seen the world. And here, boy—[*To a Page.*] Set me a stoup of wine in the oriel-room, and another for this good monk.

Con. Pardon me, blessedness—but holy rule—

Bishop. Oh! I forgot.—A pail of water and a peck of beans for the holy man!—Order up my equerry, and bid my armourer—vestryman, I mean—look out my newest robes—Plague on this gout!

[*Exeunt, following the Bishop.*

SCENE IV.

The Nave of Bamberg Cathedral. A Procession entering the West Door, headed by ELIZABETH *and the Bishop, Nobles, &c. religiously bearing the Coffin which incloses* LEWIS'S *Bones.*

1*st Lady.* See! the procession comes—the mob streams in
At every door. Hark! how the steeples thunder
Their solemn base above the wailing choir.

2*d Lady.* They will stop at the screen.

Knight. And there, as I hear, open the coffin. Push forward, ladies, to that pillar: thence you will see all.

1*st Peas.* Oh dear! oh dear! If any man had told me that I should ride forty miles on this errand, to see him that went out flesh come home grass, like the flower of the field!

2d Peas. We have changed him, but not mended him, say I, friend.

1st Peas. Never we. He knew where a yeoman's heart lay! One that would clap a man on the back when his cow died, and behave like a gentleman to him—that never met you after a hailstorm without lightening himself of a few pocket-burners.

2d Peas. Ay, that's your poor man's plaster: that's your right grease for the world's creaking wheels.

1st Peas. Nay, that's your rich man's plaster too, and covers the multitude of sins. That's your big pike's swimming-bladder, that keeps him atop and feeding: that's his calling and election, his oil of anointing, his *salvum fac regem,* his yeomen of the wardrobe, who keeps the velvet-piled side of this world uppermost, lest his delicate eyes should see the warp that holds it.

2d Peas. Who's the warp, then?

1st Peas. We, man, the friezes and fustians, that rub on till we get frayed through with overwork, and then all's abroad, and the nakedness of Babylon is discovered, and catch who catch can.

Old Woman. Pity they only brought his bones home! He would have made a lovely corpse, surely. He was a proper man!

1st Lady. Oh the mincing step he had with him! and the delicate hand on a horse, fingering the reins as St. Cicely does the organ-keys!

2d Lady. And for hunting, and another Siegfried.

Knight. If he was Siegfried the gay, she was Chriemhild the grim; and as likely to prove a firebrand as the girl in the ballad.

1*st Lady.* Gay, indeed! His smiles were like plumcake, the sweeter the deeper iced. I never saw him speak civil word to woman, but to her.

2*d Lady.* Oh, ye Saints! There was honey spilt on the ground! If I had such a knight, I'd never freeze alone on the chamber-floor, like some that never knew when they were well off. I'd never elbow him off to crusades with my pruderies.

"Pluck your apples while they 're ripe,
And pull your flowers in May, O!"

Eh! Mother?

Old Woman. "Till when she grew wizened, and he grew cold,
The balance lay even 'twixt young and old."

Monk. Thus Satan bears witness perforce against the vanities of Venus! But what 's this babbling? Carolationes in the holy place? Tace, vetula! taceas, taceto also, and that forthwith.

Old Woman. Tace in your teeth, and taceas also, begging box! Who put the halter round his waist to keep it off his neck, who? Get behind your screen, sirrah! Am I not a burgher's wife? Am I not in the nave? Am I not on my own ground? Have I brought up eleven children, without nurse, wet or dry, to be taced now-a-days by friars in the nave? Help! good folks! Where be these rooks a going?

Knight. The monk has vanished.

1st Peas. It's ill letting out waters, he finds. Who is that old gentleman, sir, holds the Princess so tight by the hand?

Knight. Her uncle, knave, the Bishop.

1st Peas. Very right, he: for she's a'most a born natural, poor soul. It was a temptation to deal with her.

2d Peas. Thou didst cheat her shockingly, Frank, time o' the famine, on those nine sacks of maslin meal,

Knight. Go tell her of it, rascal, and she'll thank you for it, and give you a shilling for helping her to a "cross."

Old Woman. Taceing free women in the nave! This comes of your princesses, that turn the world upside down, and demean themselves to hob and nob with these black baldicoots!

Eliz. [*In a low voice.*] I saw all Israel scattered on the hills
As sheep that have no shepherd! Oh, my people!
Who crowd with greedy eyes round this my jewel,
Poor ivory, token of his outward beauty—
Oh! had ye known his spirit!—Let his wisdom
Inform your light hearts with that Saviour's likeness
For whom he died! So had ye kept him with you;
And from the coming evils gentle Heaven
Had not withdrawn the righteous: 'tis too late!

1st Lady. There now, she smiles; do you think she ever loved him?

Knight. Never creature, but mealy-mouthed inquisitors, and shaven singing birds. She looks now as glad to be rid of him as any colt broke loose.

1st Lady. What will she do now, when this farce is over?

2d Lady. Found an abbey, that's the fashion, and elect herself abbess—set up the first week for queen-of-all-souls—tyrannize over hysterical girls, who are forced to thank her for making them miserable, and so die a saint.

Knight. Will you pray to her, my fair queen?

2d Lady. Not I, sir; the old Saints send me lovers enough, and to spare—yourself for one.

1st Lady. There is the giant-killer slain. But see—they have stopped: who is that raising the coffin lid?

2d Lady. Her familiar spirit, Conrad the heretic-catcher.

Knight. I do defy him! Thou art my only goddess;
My saint, my idol, my—ahem!

1st Lady. That well's run dry.
Look, how she trembles—Now she sinks, all shivering
Upon the pavement—Why, you'll see nought there
Flirting behind the pillar—Now she rises—
And choking down that proud heart, turns to the altar—
Her hand upon the coffin.

Eliz. I thank thee, gracious Lord, who hast fulfilled
Thine handmaid's mighty longings, with the sight
Of my beloved's bones, and dost vouchsafe
This consolation to the desolate.
I grudge not, Lord, the victim which we gave Thee,
Both he and I, of his most precious life,
To aid Thine holy city: though Thou knowest

His sweetest presence was to this world's joy
As sunlight to the taper—Oh! hadst Thou spared—
Had Thy great mercy let us, hand in hand,
Have toiled through houseless shame, on beggar's dole,
I had been blest: Thou hast him, Lord, Thou hast him—
Do with us what Thou wilt! If at the price
Of this one silly hair, in spite of Thee,
I could reclothe these wan bones with his manhood,
And clasp to my shrunk heart my hero's self—
I would not give it!
I will weep no more—
Lead on, most holy; on the sepulchre
Which stands beside the choir, lay down your burden.
[*To the People.*
Now, gentle hosts, within the close hard by,
Will we our court, as queen of sorrows, hold—
The green graves underneath us, and above
The all-seeing vault, which is the eye of God,
Judge of the widow and the fatherless.
There will I plead my children's wrongs, and there,
If as I think, there boil within your veins
The deep sure currents of your race's manhood,
Ye 'll nail the orphans' badge upon your shields,
And own their cause for God's. We name our champions—
Rudolf, the Cupbearer, Leutolf of Erlstetten,
Hartwig of Erba, and our loved Count Walter,
Our nights and vassals, sojourners among you.
Follow us. [*Exit* ELIZABETH, *&c.; the crowd following.*

ACT IV.

SCENE I.

Night. The Church of a Convent. ELIZABETH, CONRAD GERARD, MONKS, *an* ABBESS, NUNS, *&c., in the distance.*

Conrad. What 's this new weakness? At your own request
We come to hear your self-imposed vows——
And now you shrink: where are the highflown fancies
Which but last week, beside your husband's bier,
You vapoured forth? Will you become a jest?
You might have counted this tower's cost, before
You blazoned thus your plans abroad.

Eliz. Oh, spare me!

Con. Spare? Spare yourself; and spare big easy words,
Which prove your knowledge greater than your grace.

Eliz. Is there no middle path? No way to keep
My love for them, and God, at once unstained?

Con. If this were God's world, madam, and not the devil's,
It might be done.

Eliz. God's world, man? Why, God made it—
The faith asserts it God's.

Con. Potentially—
As every christened rogue 's a child of God,

Or those old hags, Christ's brides—Think of your horn-
book—
The world, the flesh, and the devil—a goodly leash!
And yet God made all three. I know the fiend,
And you should know the world—be sure, be sure,
The flesh is not a stork among the cranes.
Our nature, even in Eden gross and vile,
And by miraculous grace alone upheld,
Is now itself, and foul, and damned, must die
Ere we can live; let halting worldlings, madam,
Maunder against earth's ties, yet clutch them still.

Eliz. And yet God gave them to me—

Con. In the world;
Your babes are yours according to the flesh;
How can you hate the flesh, and love its fruit?

Eliz. The Scripture bids me love them.

Con. Truly so,
While you are forced to keep them; when God's mercy
Doth from the flesh and world deliverance offer,
Letting you bestow them elsewhere, then your love
May cease with his own usefulness, and the spirit
Range in free battle lists; I'll not waste reasons—
We'll leave you, madam, to the Spirit's voice.

[CONRAD *and* GERARD *withdraw.*

Eliz. [*Alone.*] Give up his children? Why, I'd not
give up
A lock of hair, a glove his hand had hallowed:
And they are his gift; his pledge; his flesh and blood;
Tossed off for my ambition! Ah! my husband!

His ghost's sad eyes upbraid me! Spare me, spare me!
I'd love thee still, if I dared; but I fear God.
And shall I never more see loving eyes
Look into mine, until my dying day?
That's this world's bondage: Christ would have me free,
And 'twere a pious deed to cut myself
The last, last strand, and fly: but whither? whither?
What if I cast away the bird i' the hand
And found none in the bush? 'Tis possible—
What right have I to arrogate Christ's bride-bed?
Crushed, widowed, sold to traitors? I, o'er whom
His billows and His storms are sweeping? God's not angry:
No, not so much as we with buzzing fly;
Or in the moment of His wrath's awakening
We should be—nothing. No—there's worse than that—
What if He but sat still, and let me be?
And these deep sorrows, which my vain conceit
Calls chastenings—meant for me—my ailments' cure—
Were lessons for some angels far away,
And I the corpus vile for the experiment?
The grinding of the sharp and pitiless wheels
Of some high Providence, which had its mainspring
Ages ago, and ages hence its end?
That were too horrible!—
To have torn up all the roses from my garden,
And planted thorns instead; to have forged my griefs,
And hugged the griefs I dared not forge; made earth
A hell, for hope of heaven; and after all,

These homeless moors of life toiled through, to wake,
And find blank nothing! Is that angel-world
A gaudy window, which we paint ourselves
To hide the dead void night beyond? The present?
Why here 's the present—like this arched gloom,
It hems our blind souls in, and roofs them over
With adamantine vault, whose only voice
Is our own wild prayers' echo: and our future?——
It rambles out in endless aisles of mist,
The further still the darker—Oh, my Saviour!
My God! where art Thou! That 's but a tale about
Thee,
That crucifix above—it does but show Thee
As Thou wast once, but not as Thou art now—
Thy grief, but not Thy glory: where 's that gone?
I see it not without me, and within me
Hell reigns, not Thou!

[*Dashes herself down on the altar steps.*

* * * * * *

[MONKS *in the distance chanting.*]

"Kings' daughters were among thine honourable
women"—

Eliz. Kings' daughters! I am one!

* * * * * *

Monks. "Hearken, oh daughter, and consider; incline
thine ear:
Forget also thine own people, and thy father's house,
So shall the King have pleasure in thy beauty:
For He is Thy Lord God, and worship thou Him."

Eliz. [*Springing up.*] I will forget them!
They stand between my soul and its allegiance.
Thou art my God: what matter if Thou love me?
I am Thy bond-slave, purchased with Thy life-blood;
I will remember nothing, save that debt.
Do with me what thou wilt. Alas, my babies!
He loves them—they 'll not need me.

CONRAD *advancing.*

Con. How now, madam?
Have these your prayers unto a nobler will
Won back that wandering heart?
Eliz. God's will is spoken:
The flesh is weak; the spirit 's fixed, and dares,—
Stay! confess, sir,
Did not yourself set on your brothers here
To sing me to your purpose?
Con. As I live
I meant it not; yet had I bribed them to it,
Those words were no less God's.
Eliz. I know it, I know it;
And I'll obey them: come, the victim 's ready.

[*Lays her hand on the altar.* GERARD, ABBESS, *and* MONKS *descend and advance.*]

All worldly goods and wealth, which once I loved
I now do count but dross: and my beloved,
The children of my womb, I now regard
As if they were another's, God is witness.
My pride is to despise myself; my joy

All insults, sneers, and slanders of mankind;
No creature now I love, but God alone.
Oh to be clear, clear, clear, of all but Him!
Lo, here I strip me of all earthly helps—
[*Tearing off her clothes.*
Naked and barefoot through the world to follow
My naked Lord—And for my filthy pelf—
Con. Stop, madam—
Eliz. Why so, sir?
Con. Upon thine oath!
Thy wealth is God's not thine—How darest renounce
The trust He lays on thee? I do command thee,
Being, as Aaron, in God's stead, to keep it
Inviolate, for the Church and thine own needs.
Eliz. Be it so—I have no part nor lot in 't—
There—I have spoken.
Abbess. Oh, noble soul! which neither gold, nor love,
Nor scorn can bend!
Gerard. And think what pure devotions,
What holy prayers must they have been, whose guerdon
Is such a flood of grace!
Nuns. What love again,
What flame of charity, which thus prevails
In virtue's guest!
Eliz. Is self-contempt learnt thus?
I'll home.
Abbess. And yet how blest, in these cool shades
To rest with us, as in a land-locked pool,
Touched last and lightest by the ruffling breeze.

Eliz. No! no! no! no! I will not die in the dark:
I'll breathe the free fresh air until the last,
Were it but a month—I have such things to do—
Great schemes—brave schemes—and such a little time!
Though now I am harnessed light as any foot-page.
Come, come, my ladies. [*Exeunt* ELIZABETH, &c.
Ger. Alas! poor lady!
Con. Why alas, my son!
She longs to die a saint, and here 's the way to it.
Ger. Yet why so harsh? why with remorseless knife
Home to the stem prune back each bough and bud?
I thought, the task of education was
To strengthen, not to crush; to train and feed
Each subject toward fulfilment of its nature,
According to the mind of God, revealed
In laws, congenital with every kind
And character of man.
Con. A heathen dream!
Young souls but see the gay and warm outside,
And work but in the shallow upper soil.
Mine deeper, and the sour and barren rock
Will stop you soon enough. Who trains God's saints,
He must transform, not pet—Nature 's corrupt throughout—
A gaudy snake, which must be crushed, not tamed,
A cage of unclean birds, deceitful ever;
Born in the likeness of the fiend, which Adam
Did at the Fall, the Scripture saith, put on.
Canst thou draw our Leviathan with a hook,

To make him sport for thy maidens? Scripture saith
Who is the prince of this world—so forget not.

Ger. Forgive, if my more weak and carnal judgment
Be startled by your doctrines, and doubt trembling
The path whereon you force yourself and her.

Con. Startled! Belike—belike—let doctrines be;
Thou shalt be judged by thy works; so see to them,
And let divines split hairs: dare all thou canst;
Be all thou darest;—that will keep thy brains full.
Have thy tools ready, God will find thee work—
Then up, and play the man. Fix well thy purpose—
Let one idea, like an orbed sun,
Rise radiant in thine heaven; and then round it
All doctrines, forms, and disciplines will range
As dim parhelia, or as needful clouds,
Needful, but mist-begotten, to be dashed
Aside, when fresh shall serve thy purpose better.

Ger. How? dashed aside?

Con. Yea, dashed aside—why not?
The truths, my son, are safe in God's abysses—
While we patch up the doctrines to look like them.
The best are tarnished mirrors—clumsy bridges,
Whereon, as on firm soil, the mob may walk
Across the gulf of doubt, and know no danger.
We, who see heaven, may see the hell which girds it.
Blind trust for them. When I came here from Rome,
Among the Alps, all through one frost-bound dawn,
Waiting with sealed lips the noisy day,
I walked upon a marble mead of snow—

An angel's spotless plume, laid there for me:
Then from the hill-side, in the melting noon,
Looked down the gorge, and lo! no bridge, no snow—
But seas of writhing glacier, gashed and scored
With splintered gulfs, and fathomless crevasses,
Blue lips of hell, which sucked down roaring rivers
The fiends who fled the sun. The path of Saints
Is such; so shall she look from heaven, and see
The road which led her thither. Now we'll go,
And find some lonely cottage for her lodging;
Her shelter now is but a crumbling ruin
Roofed in with pine boughs—discipline more healthy
For soul, than body: She's not ripe for death.

[*Exeunt.*

SCENE II.

Open space in a Suburb of Marpurg, near ELIZABETH'S *Hut.* COUNT WALTER *and* COUNT PAMA OF HUNGARY *entering.*

C. Pama. I have prepared my nerves for a shock.

C. Wal. You are wise, for the world's upside down here. The last gateway brought us out of Christendom into the new Jerusalem, the Fifth Monarchy, where the Saints possess the earth. Not a beggar here but has his pockets full of fair ladies' tokens: not a barefooted friar but rules a princess.

C. Pama. Creeping, I opine, into widows' houses, and for a pretence making long prayers.

C. Wal. Don't quote Scripture here, sir, especially in that gross literal way! The new lights here have taught us that Scripture's saying one thing, is a certain proof that it means another. Except, by the bye, in one text.

C. Pama. What 's that?

C. Wal. "Ask, and it shall be given you."

C. Pama. Ah! So we are to take nothing literally, and they may take literally every thing themselves?

C. Wal. Humph! As for your text, see if they do not saddle it on us before the day is out, as glibly as ever you laid it on them. Here comes the lady's tyrant, of whom I told you.

CONRAD *advances from the Hut.*

Con. And what may Count Walter's valour want here? [COUNT WALTER *turns his back.*

C. Pama. I come, sir priest, from Andreas, king renowned
Of Hungary, ambassador unworthy
Unto the Landgravine, his saintly daughter;
And fain would be directed to her presence.

Con. That is as I shall choose. But I'll not stop you.
I do not build with straw. I'll trust my pupils
To worldlings' honeyed tongues, who make long prayers,
And enter widows' houses for pretence.
There dwells the lady, who has chosen too long
The better part, to have it taken from her.
Besides that with strange dreams and revelations
She has of late been edified.

C. Wal. Bah! but they will serve your turn—and hers.

Con. What do you mean?

C. Wal. When you have cut her off from child and friend, and even Isentrudis and Guta, as I hear, are thrust out by you to starve, and she sits there, shut up like a bear in a hole, to feed on her own substance; if she has not some of these visions to look at, how is she, or any other of your poor self-gorged prisoners, to help fancying herself the only creature on earth?

Con. How now? Who more than she, in faith and practice, a living member of the Communion of Saints? Did she not lately publicly dispense in charity in a single day five hundred marks and more? Is it not my continual labour to keep her from utter penury through her extravagance in almsgiving? For whom does she take thought but for the poor, on whom, day and night, she spends her strength? Does she not tend them from the cradle, nurse them, kiss their sores, feed them, bathe them, with her own hands, clothe them, living and dead, with garments, the produce of her own labour? Did she not of late take into her own house a paralytic boy, whose loathsomeness had driven away every one else? And now that we have removed that charge, has she not with her a leprous boy, to whose necessities she ministers hourly, by day and night? What valley but blesses her for some school, some chapel, some convent, built by her munificence? Are not the hospices, which she has founded in divers towns, the wonder of Germany?—wherein she daily feeds and houses a multitude of the infirm poor of Christ? Is she not followed at every step by the blessings of the poor? Are not her hourly intercessions for the souls and bodies of all around incessant, world-famous, mighty to save? While she lives only for the Church of Christ, will you accuse her of selfish isolation?

C. Wal. I tell you, monk, if she were not healthier by God's making than ever she will be by yours, her charity would be by this time double-distilled selfishness; the mouths she fed, cupboards to store good works in; the backs she warmed, clothes'-horses to hang out her wares before God; her alms not given, but fairly paid, a halfpenny for every halfpenny-worth of eternal life; earth her chess-board, and the men and women on it, merely pawns for her to play a winning game—puppets and horn-books to teach her unit holiness—a private workshop in which to work out her own salvation. Out upon such charity!

Con. God hath appointed that our virtuous deeds—
Each merit their rewards.

C. Wal. Go to—go to. I have watched you and your crew, how you preach up selfish ambition for divine charity, and call prurient longings celestial love, while you blaspheme that very marriage from whose mysteries you borrow all your cant. The day will come when every husband and father will hunt you down like vermin; and may I live to see it.

Con. Out on thee, heretic!

C. Wal. (Drawing.) Liar! At last!

C. Pama. In God's name, sir, what if the Princess find us?

C. Wal. Ay—for her sake. But put that name on me

again, as you do on every good Catholic who will not be your slave and puppet, and if thou goest home with ears and nose, there is no hot blood in Germany.

[*They move toward the Cottage.*

Con. [*Alone.*] Were I as once I was, I could revenge:
But now all private grudges wane like mist
In the keen sunlight of my full intent;
And this man counts but for some sullen bull
Who paws and mutters at unheeding pilgrims
His empty wrath: yet let him bar my path,
Or stay me but one hour in my life-purpose,
And I will fell him as a savage beast,
God's foe, not mine. Beware thyself, Sir Count!

[*Exit. The Counts return from the Cottage.*

C. Pama. Shortly she will return; here to expect her
Is duty both, and honour. Pardon me—
Her humours are well known here? Passers by
Will guess who 'tis we visit?

C. Wal. Very likely.

C. Pama. Well, travellers see strange things—and do them too.
Hem! this turf-smoke affects my breath: we might
Draw back a space.

C. Wal. Certie, we were in luck,
Or both our noses would have been snapped off
By those two she-dragons; how their sainthoods squealed
To see a brace of beards peep in! Poor child!
Two sweet companions for her loneliness!

C. Pama. But ah! what lodging! 'Tis at that my heart bleeds!
That hut, whose rough and smoke-embrowned spars
Dip to the cold clay floor on either side!
Her seats bare deal!—her only furniture
Some earthern crock or two! Why, sir, a dungeon
Were scarce more frightful: such a choice must argue
Aberrant senses, or degenerate blood?

C. Wal. What? Were things foul?

C. Pama. I marked not, sir.

C. Wal. I did.
You might have eat your dinner off the floor.

C. Pama. Off any spot, sir, which a princess's foot
Had hallowed by its touch.

C. Wal. Most courtierly.
Keep, keep, those sweet saws for the lady's self.
[*Aside.*] Unless that shock of the nerves shall send them flying.

C. Pama. Yet whence this depth of poverty? I thought
You and her champions had recovered for her
Her lands and titles.

C. Wal. Ay; that coward Henry
Gave them all back as lightly as he took them:
Certie, we were four gentle applicants—
And Rudolph told him some unwelcome truths—
Would God that all of us might hear our sins,
As Henry heard that day!

C. Pama. Then she refused them?

C. Wal. "It ill befits," quoth she, "my royal blood,
To take extorted gifts; I tender back
By you to him, for this his mortal life,
That which he thinks by treason cheaply bought;
To which my son shall, in his father's right,
By God's good will, succeed. For that dread height
May Christ by many woes prepare his youth!"

C. Pama. Humph!

C. Wal. Why here—no, 't cannot be—

C. Pama. What hither comes
Forth from the hospital, where, as they told us,
The Princess labours in her holy duties?
A particoloured ghost that stalks for penance?
Ah! a good head of hair, if she had kept it
A thought less lank; a handsome face too, trust me,
But worn to fiddle strings; well, we'll be knightly—

[*As* ELIZABETH *meets him.*]

Stop, my fair queen of rags and patches, turn
Those solemn eyes a moment from your distaff,
And say, what tidings your magnificence
Can bring us of the Princess?

Eliz. I am she.

[COUNT PAMA *crosses himself and falls on his knees.*]

C. Pama. Oh blessed saints and martyrs! Open, earth!
And hide my recreant knighthood in thy gulf!
Yet mercy, madam! for till this strange day
Who e'er saw spinning wool, like village-maid,
A royal scion?

C. Wal. [*Kneeling.*] My beloved mistress!

Eliz. Ah! faithful friend! Rise, gentles, rise, for shame;
Nay, blush not, gallant sir. You have seen, ere now,
Kings' daughters do worse things than spinning wool,
Yet never reddened. Speak your errand out.

C. Pama. I from your father, madam—

Eliz. Oh! I divine;
And grieve that you so far have journeyed, sir,
Upon a bootless quest.

C. Pama. But hear me, madam—
If you return with me (o'erwhelming honour!
For such mean body-guard too precious treasure)
Your father offers to you half his wealth;
And countless hosts, whose swift and loyal blades
From traitorous grasp shall vindicate your crown.

Eliz. Wealth? I have proved it, and have tossed it from me:
I will not stoop again to load with clay.
War? I have proved that too: should I turn loose
On these poor sheep the wolf whose fangs have gored me,
God's bolt would smite me dead.

C. Pama. Madam, by his gray hairs he doth entreat you.

Eliz. Alas! small comfort would they find in me!
I am a stricken and most luckless deer,
Whose bleeding track but draws the hounds of wrath
Where'er I pause a moment. He has children
Bred at his side, to nurse him in his age—

While I am but an alien and a changeling,
Whom, ere my plastic sense could impress take
Either of his feature or his voice, he lost.

C. Pama. Is it so? Then pardon, madam, but your father
Must by a father's right command—

Eliz. Command! Ay, that 's the phrase of the world:—well—tell him,
But tell him gently too—that child and father
Are names, whose earthly sense I have foresworn,
And know no more: I have a heavenly spouse,
Whose service doth all other claims annul.

C. Wal. Ah lady, dearest lady, be but ruled!
Your Saviour will be there as near as here.

Eliz. What? Thou too, friend? Dost thou not know me better?
Wouldst have me leave undone what I begin?
[*To* COUNT PAMA.] My father took the cross, sir: so did I:
As he would die at his post, so will I die:
He is a warrior: ask him, should I leave
This my safe fort, and well-proved vantage-ground,
To roam on this world's flat and fenceless steppes?

C. Pama. Pardon me, madam, if my grosser wit
Fail to conceive your sense.

Eliz. It is not needed.
Be but the mouthpiece to my father, sir;
And tell him—for I would not anger him—
Tell him, I am content—say, happy—tell him

I prove my kin by prayers for him, and masses
For her who bore me. We shall meet on high.
And say, his daughter is a mighty tree,
From whose wide roots a thousand sapling suckers
Drink half their life; she dare not snap the threads,
And let her offshoots wither. So farewell.
Within the convent there, as mine own guests,
You shall be fitly lodged. Come here no more.

C. Wal. C. Pama. Farewell, sweet saint! [*Exeunt.*

Eliz. May God go with you both.
No! I will win for him a nobler name,
Than captive crescents, piles of turbaned heads,
Or towns retaken from the Tartar, give.
In me he shall be greatest; my report
Shall through the ages win the quires of heaven
To love and honour him; and hinds, who bless
The poor man's patron saint, shall not forget
How she was fathered with a worthy sire. [*Exit.*

SCENE III.

Night. Interior of ELIZABETH'S *Hut. A leprous Boy sleeping on a Mattress.* ELIZABETH *watching by him.*

Eliz. My shrunk limbs, stiff from many a blow,
Are crazed with pain.
A long dim formless fog-bank creeping low,
Dulls all my brain.

I remember two young lovers,
In a golden gleam.

Across the brooding darkness shrieking hovers
That fair, foul dream.

My little children call to me,
"Mother! so soon forgot?"
From out dark nooks their yearning faces startle
me,
Go, babes! I know you not!

Pray! pray! or thou 'lt go mad.

* * * * *

The past 's our own:
No fiend can take that from us! Ah, poor boy!
Had I, like thee, been bred from my black birth-hour
In filth and shame, counting the soulless months
Only by some fresh ulcer! I'll be patient—
Here 's something yet more wretched than myself.
Sleep thou on still, poor charge—though I'll not grudge
One moment of my sickening toil about thee,
Best counsellor—dumb preacher, who dost warn me
How much I have enjoyed, how much have left,
Which thou hast never known. How am I wretched?
The happiness thou hast from me, is mine,
And makes me happy. Ay, there lies the secret—
Could we but crush that ever-craving lust
For bliss, which kills all bliss, and lose our life,
Our barren unit life, to find again
A thousand lives in those for whom we die;
So were we men and women, and should hold

Our rightful rank in God's great universe,
Wherein, in heaven and earth, by will or nature,
Nought lives for self—All, all—from crown to footstool—
The Lamb, before the world's foundations slain—
The angels, ministers to God's elect—
The sun, who only shines to light a world—
The clouds, whose glory is to die in showers—
The fleeting streams who in their ocean-graves
Flee the decay of stagnant self-content—
The oak, ennobled by the shipwright's axe—
The soil, which yields its marrow to the flower—
The flower, which feeds a thousand velvet worms,
Born, only to be prey for every bird—
All spend themselves for others: and shall man,
Earth's rosy blossom—image of his God—
Whose twofold being is the mystic knot
Which couples earth and heaven—doubly bound
As being both worm and angel, to that service
By which both worms and angels hold their life,
Shall he, whose every breath is debt on debt,
Refuse, without some hope of further wage
Which he calls Heaven, to be what God has made him?
No! let him show himself the creature's lord
By freewill gift of that self-sacrifice
Which they perforce by nature's law must suffer.
This too I had to learn, (I thank thee, Lord!)
To lie crushed down in darkness and the pit—
To lose all heart and hope—and yet to work.
What lesson could I draw from all my own woes—

Ingratitude, oppression, widowhood—
While I could hug myself in vain conceits
Of self-contented sainthood—inward raptures—
Celestial palms—and let ambition's gorge
Taint heaven, as well as earth? Is selfishness
For time, a sin—spun out to eternity
Celestial prudence? Shame! Oh, thrust me forth,
Forth, Lord, from self, until I toil and die
No more for Heaven and bliss, but duty, Lord,
Duty to Thee, although my meed should be
The hell which I deserve! [*Sleeps.*

* * * * * *

Two Women enter.

1*st Woman*, What? snoring still? 'Tis nearly time to wake her
To do her penance.

2*d Woman.* Wait awhile, for love:
Indeed, I am almost ashamed to punish
A bag of skin and bones.

1*st Woman.* 'Tis for her good:
She has had her share of pleasure in this life
With her gay husband; she must have her pain.
We bear it as a thing of course; we know
What mortifications are, although I say it
That should not.

2*d Woman.* Why, since my old tyrant died,
Fasting I've sought the Lord, like any Anna,
And never tasted fish, nor flesh, nor fowl,

And little stronger than water.

1*st Woman.* Plague on this watching!
What work, to make a saint a fine lady!
See now, if she had been some labourer's daughter,
She might have saved herself, for aught he cared;
But now—

2*d Woman.* Hush! here the master comes:
I hear him.—

CONRAD *enters.*

Con. My peace, most holy, wise, and watchful wardens!
She sleeps? Well, what complaints have you to bring
Since last we met? How? blowing up the fire?
Cold is the true Saint's element—he thrives
Like Alpine gentians, where the frost is keenest—
For there Heaven's nearest—and the ether purest—
[*Aside.*] And he most bitter.

2*d Woman.* Ah! sweet master,
We are not yet as perfect as yourself.

Con. But how has she behaved?

1*st Woman.* Just like herself—
Now ruffling up like a tourney queen;
Now weeping in dark corners; then next minute
Begging for penance on her knees.

2*d Woman.* One trick's cured;
That lust of giving; Isentrude and Guta,
The hussies, came here begging but yestreen,
Vowed they were starving.

Con. Did she give to them?

2d Woman. She told them that she dared not.

Con. Good—for them,
I will take measures that they shall not want;
But see you tell her not: she must be perfect.

1st Woman. Indeed, there 's not much chance of that awhile.
There 's others, might be saints, if they were young,
And handsome, and had titles to their names,
If they were helped toward heaven, now—

Con. Silence, horse-scull!
Thank God, that you are allowed to use a finger
Towards building up His chosen tabernacle.

2d Woman. I consider that she blasphemes the means of grace.

Con. Eh? that 's a point, indeed.

2d Woman. Why, yesterday,
Within the church, before a mighty crowd,
She mocked at all the lovely·images,
And said, "the money had been better spent
"On food and clothes, instead of paint and gilding:
They were but pictures, whose reality
We ought to bear within us."

Con. Awful doctrine!

1st Woman. Look at her carelessness, again—the distaff
Or woolcomb in her hands, even on her bed.
Then, when the work is done, she lets those nuns
Cheat her of half the price.

2d Woman. The Aldenburgers.
Con. Well, well, what more misdoings?
[*Aside.*] Pah! I am sick on 't,
[*Aloud.*] Go sit, and pray by her until she wakes.
[*The Women retire.* CONRAD *sits down by the fire.*]
I am dwindling to a peddling chamber-chaplain,
Who hunts for crabs and ballads in maids' sleeves,
I, who have shuffled kingdoms. Oh! 'tis easy
To beget great deeds; but in the rearing of them—
The threading in cool blood each mean detail,
And furzebrake of half-pertinent circumstance—
There lies the self-denial.
Women [*In a low voice.*] Master! sir! look here!
Eliz. [*rising.*] Have mercy, mercy, Lord!
Con. What is it, my daughter? No—She answers not—
Her eyeballs through their sealed lids are bursting,
And yet she sleeps: her body does but mimic
The absent soul's enfranchised wanderings
In the spirit-world.
Eliz. Oh! She was but a worldling!
And think, good Lord, if that this world is hell,
What wonder if poor souls whose lot is fixed here,
Meshed down by custom, wealth, rank, pleasure, ignorance,
Do hellish things in it? Have mercy, Lord;
Even for my sake, and all my woes, have mercy!
Con. There! she is laid again—Some bedlam dream.
So—here I sit; am I a guardian angel

Watching by God's elect? or nightly tiger,
Who waits upon a dainty point of honour
To clutch his prey, till it shall wake and move?
We'll waive that question: there's eternity
To answer that in.
How like a marble-carven nun she lies
Who prays with folded palms upon her tomb,
Until the resurrection! Fair and holy!
Oh, happy Lewis! had I been a knight—
A man at all—What's this? I must be brutal,
Or I shall love her: and yet that's no safeguard;
I have marked it oft: ay—with that devilish triumph
Which eyes its victim's writhings, still will mingle
A sympathetic thrill of lust—say, pity.

Eliz. [*Awaking.*] I am heard! She is saved!
Where am I? What, have I overslept myself?
Oh, do not beat me! I will tell you all—
I have had awful dreams of the other world.

1*st Woman.* Ay! ay! a fine excuse for lazy women,
Who cry nightmare with lying on their backs.

Eliz. I will be heard! I am a prophetess!
God hears me, why not ye?

Con. Quench not the spirit:
If He have spoken, daughter, we must listen.

Eliz. Methought from out the red and heaving earth
My mother rose, whose broad and queenly limbs
A fiery arrow did impale, and round
Pursuing tongues oozed up of nether fire,
And fastened on her: like a winter-blast

Among the steeples, then she shrieked aloud,
'Pray for me, daughter, save me from this torment,
For thou canst save!' And then she told a tale;
It was not true—my mother was not such—
Oh God! The pander to a brother's sin!
1st Woman. There now? The truth is out! I told you, sister,
About that mother—
Con. Silence, hags! What then?
Eliz. She stretched her arms, and sank. Was it a sin
To love that sinful mother? There I lay—
And in the spirit far away I prayed;
What words I spoke, I know not, nor how long;
Until a still small voice sighed, 'Child, thou art heard:'
Then on the pitchy dark a small bright cloud
Shone out, and swelled, and neared, and grew to form,
Till from it blazed my pardoned mother's face
With nameless glory? Nearer still she pressed,
And bent her lips to mine—a mighty spasm
Ran crackling through my limbs, and thousand bells
Rang in my dizzy ears—And so I woke.
Con. 'Twas but a dream.
Eliz. 'Twas more! 'twas more! I've tests:
From youth I have lived in two alternate worlds,
And night is live like day. This was no goblin!
'Twas a true vision, and my mother's soul
Is freed by my poor prayers from penal fires,
And waits for me in bliss.
Con. Well—be it so then.

Thou seest herein what prize obedience merits.
Now to press forwards: I require your presence
Within the square, at noon, to witness there
The fiery doom—most just and righteous doom—
Of two convicted and malignant heretics,
Who at the stake shall expiate their crime,
And pacify God's wrath against this land.

Eliz. No! no! I will not go!

Con. What's here? Thou wilt not?
I'll drive thee there with blows.

Eliz. Then I will bear them,
Even as I bore the last, with thankful thoughts
Upon those stripes my Lord endured for me.
Oh spare them, sir! poor blindfold sons of men!
No saint but daily errs,—and must they burn,
Ah God! for an opinion?

Con. Fool! opinions?
Who cares for their opinions? 'Tis rebellion
Against the system which upholds the world
For which they die: so, lest the infection spread,
We must cut off the members, whose disease
We'd pardon, could they keep it to themselves.

[ELIZABETH *weeps.*

Well, I'll not urge it,—Thou hast other work—
But for thy petulant words do thou this penance:
I do forbid thee here, to give henceforth
Food, coin, or clothes, to any living soul.
Thy thriftless waste doth scandalize the elect,
And maim thine usefulness: thou dost elude

My wise restrictions still: 'Tis great, to live
Poor, among riches; when thy wealth is spent,
Want is not merit, but necessity.

Eliz. Oh, let me give!
That only pleasure have I left on earth!

Con. And for that very cause thou must forego it,
And so be perfect: 'she who lives in pleasure
Is dead, while yet she lives;' grace brings no merit
When 'tis the express of our own self-will.
To shrink from what we practise; do God's work
In spite of loathings; that's the path of saints.
I have said. [*Exit, with the Women.*

Eliz. Well! I am freezing fast—I have grown of late
Too weak to nurse my sick; and now this outlet,
This one last thawing spring of fellow-feeling,
Is choked with ice—Come, Lord, and set me free.
Think me not hasty! measure not mine age,
Oh Lord, by these my four and twenty winters.
I have lived three lives—three lives.
For fourteen years I was an idiot girl:
Then I was born again; and for five years,
I lived! I lived! and then I died once more;—
One day when many knights came marching by,
And stole away—we'll talk no more of that.
And so these four years since, I have been dead,
And all my life is hid with Christ in God.
Nunc igitur dimittas, Domine, servam tuam.

SCENE IV.

The Same. ELIZABETH *lying on Straw in a corner. A crowd of Women round her.* CONRAD *entering.*

Con. As I expected—
A sermon-mongering herd about her death-bed,
Stifling her with fusty sighs, as flocks of rooks
Despatch, with pious pecks, a wounded brother.
Cant, howl, and whimper! Not an old fool in the town
Who thinks herself religious, but must see
The last of the show, and mob the deer to death.
[*Advancing.*] Hail! holy ones! How fares your charge to-day?

Abbess. After the blessed sacrament received,
As surfeited with those celestial viands,
And with the blood of life intoxicate,
She lay entranced; and only stirred at times
To eructate sweet edifying doctrine
Culled from your darling sermons.

Woman. Heavenly grace
Imbues her so throughout, that even when pricked
She feels no pain.

Con. A miracle, no doubt.
Heaven's work is ripe, and like some more I know,
Having begun in the spirit, in the flesh
She 's now made perfect: she hath had warnings, too,
Of her decease; and prophesied to me,
Three weeks ago, when I lay like to die,
That I should see her in her coffin yet.

Abbess. 'Tis said, she heard in dreams her Saviour call her
To mansions built for her from everlasting.

Con. Ay, so she said.

Abbess. But tell me, in her confession
Was there no holy shame—no self-abhorrence
For the vile pleasures of her carnal wedlock?

Con. She said no word thereon: as for her shrift,
No Chrisom child could show a chart of thoughts
More spotless than were hers.

Nun. Strange, she said nought;
I had hoped she had grown more pure.

Con. When, next, I asked her,
How she would be interred; "In the vilest weeds,"
Quoth she, "my poor hut holds; I will not pamper
When dead, that flesh, which living I despised.
And for my wealth, see it to the last doit
Bestowed upon the poor of Christ."

2d Woman. Oh grace!

3d Woman. Oh soul to this world poor, but rich toward God!

Eliz. [*Awaking.*] Hark! how they cry for bread! Poor souls! be patient!
I have spent all—
I'll sell myself for a slave—feed them with the price.
Come, Guta! Nurse! We must be up and doing!
Alas! they are gone, and begging!
Go! go! They'll beat me, if I give you aught:
I'll pray for you, and so you'll go to Heaven.

I am a saint—God grants me all I ask.
But I must love no creature. Why, Christ loved—
Mary he loved, and Martha, and their brother—
Three friends! and I have none!
When Lazarus lay dead, He groaned in spirit,
And wept—like any widow—Jesus wept!
I'll weep, weep, weep! pray for that "gift of tears."
They took my friends away, but not my eyes.
Oh, husband, babes, friends, nurse! To die alone!
Crack, frozen brain! Melt, icicle within!

Women. Alas! Sweet saint! By bitter pangs she wins
Her crown of endless glory!

Con. But she wins it!
Stop that vile sobbing: she 's unmanned enough
Without your maudlin sympathy.

Eliz. What! weeping?
Daughters of Jerusalem, weep not for me—
Weep for yourselves.

Women. We do, alas! we do!
What are we without you? [*A pause.*

Woman. Oh listen, listen!
What sweet sounds from her fast-closed lips are welling,
As from the caverned shaft, deep miners' songs?

Eliz. [*in a low voice.*] Through the stifling room
Floats strange perfume;
Through the crumbling thatch
The angels watch,
Over the rotting roof-tree.

They warble, and flutter, and hover and glide,
Wafting old sounds to my dreary bedside,
Snatches of songs which I used to know
When I slept by my nurse, and the swallows
Called me at day-dawn from under the eaves.
Hark to them! Hark to them now—
Fluting like woodlarks, tender and low—
Cool rustling leaves—tinkling waters—
Sheepbells over the lea—
In their silver plumes Eden-gales whisper—
In their hands Eden-lilies—not for me—not for me—
No crown for the poor fond bride!
The song told me so,
Long, long ago,
How the maid chose the white lily;
But the bride she chose
The red red rose,
And by its thorn died she.

Well—in my Father's house are many mansions—

I have trodden the waste howling ocean-foam,
Till I stand upon Canaan's shore,
Where Crusaders from Zion's towers call me home,
To the saints who are gone before.

Con. Still on Crusaders? [*Aside.*
Abbess. What was that sweet song, which just now, my Princess,
You murmured to yourself?

Eliz. Did you not hear
A little bird between me and the wall,
That sang and sang?
Abbess. We heard him not, fair saint.
Eliz. I heard him, and his merry carol revelled
Through all my brain, and woke my parched throat
To join his song: then angel melodies
Burst through the dull dark, and the mad air quivered
Unutterable music. Nay, you heard him.
Abbess. Nought save yourself.
Eliz. Slow hours! Was that the cock-crow?
Woman. St. Peter's bird did call.
Eliz. Then I must up—
To matins, and to work—No, my work 's over.
And what is it, what?
One drop of oil on the salt seething ocean!
Thank God, that one was born at this same hour
Who did our work for us: we 'll talk of Him:
We shall go mad with thinking of ourselves—
We 'll talk of Him, and of that new-made star,
Which, as he stooped into the Virgin's side,
From off His finger, like a signet-gem,
He dropped in the empyrean for a sign.
But the first tear He shed at this His birth-hour,
When He crept weeping forth to see our woe,
Fled up to Heaven in mist, and hid forever
Our sins, our works, and that same new-made star.
Woman. Poor soul! she wanders!
Con. Wanders, fool? her madness

Is worth a million of your paters, mumbled
At every station between—

Eliz. Oh! thank God
Our eyes are dim! What should we do, if he,
The sneering fiend, who laughs at all our toil,
Should meet us face to face?

Con. We'd call him fool.

Eliz. There! There! Fly, Satan, fly! 'Tis gone!

Con. The victory's gained at last!
The fiend is baffled, and her saintship sure!
Oh people blest of heaven!

Eliz. Oh master, master!
You will not let the mob, when I lie dead
Make me a show—paw over all my limbs—
Pull out my hair—pluck off my finger-nails—
Wear scraps of me for charms and amulets,
As if I were a mummy, or a drug?
As they have done to others—I have seen it—
Nor set me up in ugly naked pictures
In every church, that cold world-hardened wits
May gossip o'er my secret tortures? Promise—
Swear to me! I demand it!

Con. No man lights
A candle, to be hid beneath a bushel:
Thy virtues are the Church's dower: endure
All which the edification of the faithful
Makes needful to be published.

Eliz. Oh my God!
I had stripped myself of all, but modesty!

Dost thou claim yet that victim ? Be it so.
Now take me home ! I have no more to give thee !
So weak—and yet no pain—why, now nought ails me !
How dim the lights burn ! Here—
Where are you, children ?
Alas ! I had forgotten.
Now I must sleep—for ere the sun shall rise,
I must begone upon a long, long journey
To him I love.

Con. She means her heavenly bridegroom—
The spouse of souls.

Eliz. I said, to him I love.
Let me sleep, sleep.
You will not need to wake me—so—good night.

[*Folds herself into an attitude of repose. The Scene closes.*]

ACT V.

SCENE I. A.D. 1235.

A Convent at Marpurg. Cloisters of the Infirmary. Two aged MONKS *sitting.*

1*st Monk.* So they will publish to-day the Landgravine's canonization, and translate her to the new church prepared for her. Alack, now, that all the world should be out sight-seeing and saint-making, and we laid up here, like two lame jackdaws in a belfry!

2*d Monk.* Let be man—let be. We have seen sights and saints in our time. And, truly, this insolatio suits my old bones better than processioning.

1*st Monk.* 'Tis pleasant enough in the sun, were it not for the flies. Look—there 's a lizard. Come you here, little run-about; here 's game for you.

2*d Monk.* A tame fool, and a gay one—Munditiæ mundanis.

1*st Monk.* Catch him a flat fly—my hand shaketh.

2*d Monk.* If one of your new-lights were here, now, he 'd pluck him for a fiend, as Dominic did the live sparrow in chapel.

1*st Monk.* There will be precious offerings made to-day, of which our house will get its share.

2*d Monk.* Not we; she always favoured the Franciscans most.

1*st Monk.* 'Twas but fair—they were her kith and kin. She lately put on the habit of their third minors.

2*d Monk.* So have half the fine gentlemen and ladies in Europe. There 's one of your new inventions, now, for letting grand folk serve God and mammon at once, and emptying honest monasteries, where men give up all for the Gospel's sake. And now these Pharisees of Franciscans will go off with full pockets—

1*st Monk.* While we poor publicans—

2*d Monk.* Shall not come home all of us justified, I think.

1*st Monk.* How? Is there scandal among us?

2*d Monk.* Ask not—ask not. Even a fool, when he holds his peace is counted wise. Of all sins, avoid that same gossiping.

1*st Monk.* Nay, tell me now. Are we not like David and Jonathan? Have we not worked together, prayed together, journeyed together, and been soundly flogged together, more by token, any time this forty years? And now is news so plenty, that thou darest to defraud me of a morsel?

2*d Monk.* I'll tell thee—but be secret. I knew a man hard by the convent (names are dangerous, and a bird of the air shall carry the matter,) one that hath a mighty eye for a heretic, if thou knowest him.

1*st Monk.* Who carries his poll screwed on overtight, and sits with his eyes shut in chapel?

2*d Monk.* The same. Such a one to be in evil savour—to have the splendour of the pontifical countenance turned from him, as though he had taken Christians for Amalekites, and slain the people of the Lord.

1*st Monk.* How now?

2*d Monk.* I only speak as I hear: for my sister's son is chaplain, for the time being, to a certain Archisacerdos, a foreigner, now lodging where thou knowest. The young man being hid, after some knavery, behind the arras, in come our quidam and that prelate. The quidam, surly and Saxon—the guest, smooth and Italian; his words softer than butter, yet very swords: that this quidam had "exceeded the bounds of his commission—launched out into wanton and lawless cruelty—burnt noble ladies unheard, of whose innocence the Holy See had proof—defiled the Catholic faith in the eyes of the weaker sort—and alienated the minds of many nobles and gentlemen"—and finally, that he who thinketh he standeth, were wise to take heed lest he fall.

1*st Monk.* And what said Conrad?

2*d Monk.* Out upon a man that cannot keep his lips! Who spake of Conrad? That quidam, however, answered nought, but—how, "to his own master he stood or fell" —how "he laboured not for the Pope but for the Papacy;" and so forth.

1*st Monk.* Here is awful doctrine! Behold the fruit of your reformers! This comes of their realized ideas, and centralizations, and organizations, till a monk cannot wink in chapel without being blinded with the lantern, or fall sick on Fridays, for fear of the rod. Have I not testified? Have I not foretold?

2d Monk. Thou hast indeed. Thou knowest that the old paths are best, and livest in most pious abhorrence of all amendment.

1st Monk. Do you hear that shout? There is the procession returning from the tomb.

2d Monk. Hark to the tramp of the horse-hoofs! A gallant show, I'll warrant!

1st Monk. Time was, now, when we were young bloods together in the world, such a roll as that would have set our hearts beating against their cages!

2d Monk. Ay, ay. We have seen sport in our day; we have paraded and curvetted, eh? and heard scabbards jingle? We know the sly touch of the heel, that set him on his hind legs before the right window? Vanitas vanitatum—omnia vanitas! Here comes Gerard, Conrad's chaplain, with our dinner.

[GERARD *enters across the Court.*]

1st Monk. A kindly youth and a godly, but—reformation bitten, like the rest.

2d Monk. Never care. Boys must take the reigning madness in religion, as they do the measles—once for all.

1st Monk. Once too often for him. His face is too, too like Abel's in the chapel-window. Ut sis vitalis metuo, puer!

Ger. Hail, fathers. I have asked permission of the prior to minister your refection, and bring you thereby the first news of the pageant.

1st Monk. Blessings on thee for a good boy. Give us the trenchers, and open thy mouth while we open ours.

2d Monk. Most splendid all, no doubt?

Ger. A garden, sir,
Wherein all rainbowed flowers were heaped together;
A sea of silk and gold, of blazoned banners,
And chargers housed; such glorious press, be sure,
Thuringen-land ne'er saw.

2d Monk. Just hear the boy!
Who rode beside the bier?

Ger. Frederic the Kaiser,
Henry the Landgrave, brother of her husband;
The Princesses, too, Agnes, and her mother;
And every noble name, sir, at whose war-cry
The Saxon heart leaps up; with them the prelates
Of Treves, of Cöln, and Maintz—why name them all?
When all were there, whom this our father-land
Counts worthy of its love.

1st Monk. 'Twas but her right.
Who spoke the oration?

Ger. Who but Conrad?

2d Monk. Well—
That's honour to our house.

1st Monk. Come, tell us all.

2d Monk. In order, boy: thou hast a ready tongue.

Ger. He raised from off her face the pall, and "Lo!"
He cried, "That saintly flesh which ye of late
With sacrilegious hands, ere yet entombed,
Had in your superstitious selfishness
Almost torn piecemeal. Fools! Gross-hearted fools!
These limbs are God's, not yours: in life for you

They spent themselves; now till the judgment-day
By virtue of the Spirit embalmed they lie—
Touch them who dare. No! Would you find your saint,
Look up, not down, where even now she prays
Beyond that blazing orb for you and me.
Why hither bring her corpse? Why hide her clay
In jewelled ark beneath God's mercy-seat—
A speck of dust among these boundless aisles,
Uprushing pillars, star-bespangled roofs,
Whose colours mimic Heaven's unmeasured blue,
Save to remind you, how she is not here,
But risen with Him that rose, and by his blaze
Absorbed, lives in the God for whom she died?
Know her no more according to the flesh;
Or only so, to brand upon your thoughts
How she was once a woman—flesh and blood,
Like you—yet how unlike! Hark while I tell ye."

2d Monk. How liked the mob all this? They hate him sore.

Ger. Half awed, half sullen, till his golden lips
Entranced all ears with tales so sad and strange,
They seemed one life-long miracle: bliss and woe,
Honour and shame—her daring—Heaven's stern guidance,
Did each the other so outblaze.

1st Monk. Great signs
Did wait on her from youth.

2d Monk. There went a tale
Of one, a Zingar wizard, who, on her birthnight,

He here in Eisenach, she in Presburg lying,
Declared her natal moment, and the glory
Which should befall her by the grace of God.

Ger. He spoke of that, and many a wonder more,
Melting all hearts to worship—how a robe
Which from her shoulders, at a royal feast,
To some importunate as alms she sent,
By miracle within her bower was hung again:
And how on her own couch the Incarnate Son
In likeness of a leprous serf, she laid:
And many a wondrous tale, till now unheard;
Which, from her handmaid's oath and attestation,
Siegfried of Maintz to far Perugia sent,
And sainted Umbria's labyrinthine hills,
Even to the holy Council, where the Patriarchs
Of Antioch and Jerusalem, and with them
A host of prelates, magnates, knights and nobles,
Decreed and canonized her sainthood's palm.

1st Monk. Mass, they could do no less.

Ger. So thought my master——
For, " Thus," quoth he, " the primates of the Faith
Have, in the bull which late was read to you,
Most wisely ratified the will of God
Revealed in her life's splendour: for the next count—
These miracles wherewith since death she shines—
Since ye must have your signs, ere ye believe,
And since without such tests the Roman Father
Allows no saints to take their seats in heaven,
Why, there ye have them; not a friar, I find,

Or old wife in the streets, but counts some dozens
Of blind, deaf, halt, dumb, palsied, and hysterical,
Made whole at this her tomb—A corpse or two
Was raised, they say, last week: Will that content you?
Will *that* content her? Earthworms! Would ye please
the dead,
Bring sinful souls, not limping carcasses
To test her power on; which of you hath done that?
Has any glutton learnt from her to fast?
Or oily burgher dealt away his pelf?
Has any painted Jezebel in sackcloth
Repented of her vanities? Your patron?
Think ye, that spell and flame of intercession,
Melting God's iron will, which for your sakes
She purchased by long agonies, was but meant
To save your doctors' bills? If any soul
Hath been by her made holier, let it speak!"

2d Monk. Well spoken, Legate! Easier asked than
answered.

Ger. Not so, for on the moment, from the crowd
Sprang out a gay and gallant gentleman
Well known in fight and tourney, and aloud
With sobs and blushes told, how he long time
Had wallowed deep in mire of fleshly sin,
And loathed, and fell again, and loathed in vain;
Until the story of her saintly grace
Drew him unto her tomb; there long prostrate
With bitter cries he sought her, till at length
The image of her perfect loveliness

Transfigured all his soul, and from his knees
He rose new-born, and, since that blessed day,
In chastest chivalry, a spotless knight,
Maintains the widow's and the orphan's cause.

1st Monk. Well done! and what said Conrad?

Ger. Oh, he smiled,
As who should say, "'Twas but the news I looked for,"
Then, pointing to the banners borne on high,
Where the sad story of her nightly penance
Was all too truly painted—"Look!" he cried,
"'Twas thus she schooled her soft and shuddering flesh
To dare and suffer for you!—Thus she won
The ear of God for you!" Gay ladies sighed,
And stern knights wept, and growled, and wept again.
And then he told her alms, her mighty labours,
Among God's poor, the schools wherein she taught;
The babes she brought to the font, the hospitals
Founded from her own penury, where she tended
The leper and the fever-stricken serf
With meanest office; how a dying slave
Who craved in vain for milk she stooped to feed
From her own bosom——At that crowning tale
Of utter love, the dullest hearts caught fire
Contagious from his lips—the Spirit's breath
Low to the earth, like dewy-laden corn,
Bowed the ripe harvest of that mighty host;
Knees bent, all heads were bare; rich dames aloud
Bewailed their cushioned sloth; old foes held out
Long parted hands; low-murmured vows and prayers

Gained courage, till a shout proclaimed her saint,
And jubilant thunders shook the ringing air,
Till birds dropped stunned, and passing clouds bewept
With crystal drops, like sympathizing angels,
Those wasted limbs, whose sainted ivory round
Shed Eden-odours: from his royal head
The Kaiser took his crown, and on the bier
Laid the rich offering; dames tore off their jewels—
Proud nobles heaped with gold and gems her corse
Whom living they despised: I saw no more——
Mine eyes were blinded with a radiant mist—
And I ran here to tell you.

1st Monk. Oh, fair olive,
Rich with the Spirit's unction, how thy boughs
Rain balsams on us!

2d Monk. Thou didst sell thine all—
And bought'st the priceless pearl!

1st Monk. Thou holocaust of Abel
By Cain in vain despised!

2d Monk. Thou angels' playmate
Of yore, but now their judge!

Ger. Thou alabaster,
Broken at last, to fill the house of God
With rich celestial fragrance!

[*&c., &c., ad libitum.*

SCENE II.

A Room in a Convent at Mayence. CONRAD *alone.*

Con. The work is done! Diva Elizabeth!

And I have trained one saint before I die!
Yet now 'tis done, is't well done? On my lips
Is triumph: but what echo in my heart?
Alas! the inner voice is sad and dull,
Even at the crown and shout of victory.
Oh! I had hugged this purpose to my heart,
Cast by for it all ruth, all pride, all scruples;
Yet now its face, that seemed as pure as crystal,
Shows fleshly, foul, and stained with tears and gore!
We make, and moil, like children in their gardens,
And spoil with dabbled hands, our flowers i' the planting.
And yet a saint is made! Alas, those children!
Was there no gentler way? I know not any:
I plucked the gay moth from the spider's web;
What if my hasty hand have smirched its feathers?
Sure, if the whole be good, each several part
May for its private blots forgiveness gain,
As in man's tabernacle, vile elements
Unite to one fair stature. Who'll gainsay it?
The whole is good; another saint in heaven;
Another bride within the Bridegroom's arms;
And she will pray for me!—And yet what matter?
Better that I, this paltry sinful unit,
Fall fighting, crushed into the nether pit,
If my dead corpse may bridge the path to Heaven,
And damn itself, to save the souls of others.
A noble ruin: yet small comfort in it;
In it, or in aught else———
A blank dim cloud before mine inward sense

Dulls all the past: she spoke of such a cloud——
I struck her for 't, and said it was a fiend——
She 's happy now, before the throne of God——
I should be merry; yet my heart's floor sinks
As on a fast day; sure some evil bodes.
Would it were here, that I might see its eyes!
The future only is unbearable;
We quail before the rising thunderstorm
Which thrills and whispers in the stifled air,
Yet blench not, when it falls. Would it were here!

[*Pause.*]

I fain would sleep, yet dare not: all the air
Throngs thick upon me with the pregnant terror
Of life unseen, yet near. I dare not meet them,
As if I sleep I shall do——I again?
What matter what I feel, or like, or fear?
Come what God sends. Within there—Brother Gerard!

[GERARD *enters.*]

Watch here an hour, and pray.—The fiends are busy.
So—hold my hand. [*Crosses himself.*
Come on—I fear you not. [*Sleeps.*

[GERARD *sings.*]

Qui fugiens mundi gravia,
Contempsit carnis bravia,
Cupidinisque somnia,
Lucratur, perdens, omnia.

Hunc gestant ulnis angeli,
Ne lapis officiat pedi;

Ne luce timor occupet,
Aut nocte pestis incubet.

Huic cœli lilia germinant;
Arrisus sponsi permanent;
Ac nomen in fidelibus
Quam filiorum melius. [*Sleeps.*]

* * * * * *

[CONRAD *awaking.*] Stay! Spirits, stay! Art thou a hell-born phantasm,
Or word too true, sent by the mother of God?
Oh tell me, queen of Heaven!
Oh God! if she, the city of the Lord,
Who is the heart, the brain, the ruling soul
Of half the earth; wherein all kingdoms, laws,
Authority, and faith do culminate,
And draw from her their sanction and their use;
The lighthouse founded on the rock of ages,
Whereto the Gentiles look, and still are healed;
The tree whose rootlets drink of every river,
Whose boughs drop Eden fruits on seaward isles;
Christ's seamless coat, rainbowed with gems and hues
Of all degrees and uses, rend, and tarnish,
And crumble into dust!
Vanitas vanitatum, omnia vanitas!
Oh! to have prayed, and toiled——and lied—for this!
For this to have crushed out the heart of youth,
And sat by calm, while living bodies burned!

How? Gerard; sleeping?
Couldst thou not watch with me one hour, my son?

Ger. [*awaking.*] How! have I slept? Shame on my vaporous brain!
And yet there crept along my hand from thine
A leaden languor, and the drowsy air
Teemed thick with humming wings—I slept perforce.
Forgive me (while for breach of holy rule
Due penance shall seem honour) my neglect.

Con. I should have beat thee for 't, an hour agone—
Now I judge no man; What are rules and methods?
I have seen things which make my brain-sphere reel:
My magic teraph-bust, full packed and labelled,
With saws, ideas, dogmas, ends, and theories,
Lies shivered into dust: Pah! we do squint
Each through his loophole, and then dream, broad heaven
Is but the patch we see. But let none know;
Be silent, Gerard, wary.

Ger. Nay—I know naught
Of that which moves thee: though I fain would ask—

Con. I saw our mighty Mother, Holy Church,
Sit like a painted harlot; round her limbs
An oily snake had coiled, who smiled, and smiled,
And lisped the name of Jesus—I'll not tell thee:
I have seen more than man can see, and live:
God, when He grants the tree of knowledge, bans
The luckless seer from off the tree of life,
Lest he become as gods, and burst with pride;

Or sick at sight of his own nothingness,
Lie down, and be a fiend: my time is near.
Well—I have neither child, nor kin, nor friend,
Save thee, my son; I shall go lightly forth.
Thou knowest, we start for Marpurg on the morrow?
Thou wilt go with me?

Ger. Ay, to death, my master;
Yet boorish heretics, with grounded throats,
Mutter like sullen bulls; the Count of Saym,
And many gentlemen, they say, have sworn
A fearful oath: there 's danger in the wind.

Con. They have their quarrel; I was keen and hasty:
Gladio qui utitur, peribit gladio.
When Heaven is strong, then Hell is strong: Thou fear'st not?

Ger. No! though their name were legion! 'Tis for thee
Alone I quake, lest by some pious boldness
Thou quench the light of Israel.

Con. Light? my son!
There shall no light be quenched, when I lie dark.
Our path trends outward: we will forth to-morrow:
Now let 's to chapel; matin bells are ringing. [*Exeunt.*

SCENE III.

A road between Eisenach and Marpurg. Peasants waiting by the road-side. WALTER OF VARILA, *the* COUNT OF SAYM, *and other Gentlemen, entering on horseback.*

Gent. Talk not of honour—Hell 's a-flame within me:
Foul water quenches fire as well as fair;

If I do meet him, he shall die the death,
Come fair, come foul: I tell you, there are wrongs
The fumbling piecemeal law can never touch,
Which bring of themselves to the injured, right divine,
Straight from the fount of right, above all parchments,
To be their own avengers: dainty lawyers,
If one shall slay the adulterer in the act,
Dare not condemn him: girls have stabbed their tyrants,
And common sense has crowned them saints; yet what—
What were their wrongs to mine? All gone! All gone!
My noble boys, whom I had trained, poor fools,
To win their spurs, and ride afield with me!
I could have spared them—but my wife! my lady!
Those dainty limbs, which knew no eyes but mine—
Before that ruffian mob—Too much for man!
Too much, stern Heaven!—Those eyes, those hands,
Those tender feet, where I have lain and worshipped—
Food for fierce flames! And on the self same day—
The day that they were seized—unheard—unargued—
No witness, but one vile convicted thief—
The dog is dead and buried: Well done, henchmen!
They are not buried! Pah! their ashes flit
About the common air; we pass them—breathe them!
The self-same day! If I had had one look!
One word—one single tiny spark of word,
Such as two swallows change upon the wing!
She was no heretic: she knelt forever
Before the blessed rood, and prayed for me.
Art sure he comes this road?

C. Saym. My messenger
Saw him start forth, and watched him past the cross-
ways:
An hour will bring him here.

C. Wal. How? ambuscading?
I'll not sit by, while helpless priests are butchered;
Shame, gentles!

C. Saym. On my word, I knew not on't
Until this hour: my quarrel 's not so sharp,
But I may let him pass: my name is righted
Before the Emperor, from all his slanders;
And what 's revenge to me?

Gent. Ay, ay—forgive and forget—
The vermin 's trapped—and we 'll be gentle-handed,
And lift him out, and bid his master speed him,
Him and his firebrands. He shall never pass me.

C. Wal. I will not see it; I'm old, and sick of blood.
She loved him, while she lived; and charged me once,
As her sworn liegeman, not to harm the knave.
I'll home; yet, knights, if aught untoward happen,
And you should need a shelter, come to me:
My walls are strong. Home, knaves! we 'll seek our
wives,
And beat our swords to ploughshares—when folks let us.

[*Exeunt* COUNT WALTER *and Suite.*

C. Saym. He 's gone, brave heart! But—sir, you
will not dare?
The Pope's own legate—think—there 's danger in 't.

Gent. Look, how athwart yon sullen sleeping flats

That frowning thunder-cloud sails pregnant hither;—
And black against its sheeted gray, one bird
Flags fearful onward—'Tis his cursed soul!
Now thou shalt quake, raven!—The self-same day!—
He cannot 'scape! The storm is close upon him?
There! There! the wreathing spouts have swallowed
him!
He 's gone! and see, the keen blue spark leaps out
From crag to crag, and every vaporous pillar
Shouts forth his death-doom! 'Tis a sign, a sign!

[*A heretic preacher mounts a stone.—Peasants gather round him.*]

These are starved unlettered hinds, forsooth,
He hunted down like vermin—for a doctrine.
They have their rights, their wrongs; their lawless laws,
Their witless arguings, which unconscious reason
Informs to just conclusions. We will hear them.

Preacher. My brethren, I have a message to you: therefore hearken with all your ears—for now is the day of salvation. It is written, that the children of this world are in their generation wiser than the children of light—and truly: for the children of this world, when they are troubled with vermin, catch them—and hear no more of them. But you, the children of light, the elect saints, the poor of this world rich in faith, let the vermin eat your lives out, and then fall down and worship them afterwards. You are all besotted—hag-ridden—drunkards sitting in the stocks, and bowing down to the said stocks, and making a god thereof. Of part, saith the prophet, ye make a god, and part serveth to roast—to roast the flesh of your sons and of your daughters; and then ye cry, "Aha, I am warm, I have seen the fire;" and a special fire ye have seen! The ashes of your wives and of your brothers cleave to your clothes.—Cast them up to Heaven, cry aloud, and quit yourselves like men!

Gent. He speaks God's truth! We are Heaven's justicers!
Our woes anoint us kings! Peace—Hark again!—

Preacher. Therefore, as I said before—in the next place—It is written, that there shall be a two edged-sword in the hand of the saints. But the saints have but two swords—Was there a sword or shield found among ten thousand in Israel? Then let Israel use his fists, say I the preacher! For this man hath shed blood, and by man shall his blood be shed. Now behold an argument.—This man hath shed blood, even Conrad; ergo, as he saith himself, ye, if ye are men, shall shed his blood. Doth he not himself say ergo? Hath he not said ergo to the poor saints, to your sons and your daughters, whom he hath burned in the fire to Moloch? "Ergo, thou art a heretic"—"Ergo, thou shalt burn." Is he not therefore convicted out of his own mouth? Arise therefore, be valiant—for this day he is delivered into your hand!

[*Chanting heard in the distance.*]

Peasant. Hush! here the psalm-singers come!

[CONRAD *enters on a mule, chanting the psalter,* GERARD *following.*]

Con. My peace with you, my children!

1st Voice. Psalm us no psalms; bless us no devil's
blessings:
Your balms will break our heads.

[*A murmur rises.*

2d Voice. You are welcome, sir; we are a-waiting for you.

3d Voice. Has he been shriven to-day?

4th Voice. Where is your ergo, Master Conrad? Faugh!
How both the fellows smell of smoke!

5th Voice. A strange leech he, to suck, and suck, and suck,
And look no fatter for 't!

Old Woman. Give me back my sons!

Old Man. Give me back the light of mine eyes,
Mine only daughter!
My only one! He hurled her over the cliffs!
Avenge me, lads, you are young!

4th Voice. We will, we will: why smit'st him not, thou with the pole-axe?

3d Voice. Nay, now, the first blow costs most, and heals last:
Besides, the dog 's a priest, at worst.

C. Saym. Mass! How the shaveling rascal stands at bay!
There 's not a rogue of them dare face his eye!
True Domini canis! 'Ware the bloodhound's teeth, curs!

Preacher. What! Are ye afraid? The huntsman 's here at last

Without his whip! Down with him, craven hounds!
I'll help ye to 't. [*Springs from the stone.*

Gent. Ay, down with him! Mass, have these yelping boors
More heart than I? [*Spurs his horse forward.*

Mob. A knight! a champion!

Voice. He 's not mortal man!
See how his eyes shine! 'Tis the archangel!
St. Michael come to the rescue! Ho! St. Michael!

[*He lunges at* CONRAD. GERARD *turns the lance aside, and throws his arms round* CONRAD.]

Ger. My master! my master! The chariot of Israel and the horses thereof!
Oh call down fire from Heaven!

[*A Peasant strikes down* GERARD. CONRAD, *over the body.*]

Alas! my son! This blood shall cry for vengeance
Before the throne of God!

Gent. And cry in vain!
Follow thy minion! Join Folquet in hell!

[*Bears* CONRAD *down on his lance-point.*

Con. I am the vicar of the vicar of Christ:
Who touches me, doth touch the Son of God.

[*The Mob close over him.*]

Oh God! A martyr's crown! Elizabeth! [*Dies.*

NOTES TO ACT I.

THE references, unless it be otherwise specified, are to the *Eight Books concerning Saint Elizabeth, by Dietrich the Thuringian;* in BASNAGE'S *Canisius*, Vol. IV., p. 113, (Antwerp, 1725.)

Page 31. Cf. Lib. I. § 3. Dietrich is eloquent about her youthful inclination for holy places and church doors, even when shut, and gives many real proofs of her 'sanctæ indolis,' from the very cradle.

P. 32. 'St. John's sworn maid.' Cf. Lib. I. § 4. 'She chose by lot for her patron, St. John the protector of virginity.'

P. 33. 'Fit for my princess.' Cf. Lib. I. § 2. 'He sent with his daughter vessels of gold, silver baths, jewels, *pillows all of silk.* No such things, so precious or so many, were ever seen in Thuringen land.'

Ibid. 'Most friendless.' Cf. Lib. I. §§ 5, 6. 'The courtiers used bitterly to insult her, &c. Her mother and sister-in-law, given to worldly pomp, differed from her exceedingly;' and much more concerning 'the persecutions which she endured patiently in youth.'

P. 34. 'In one cradle.' Cf. Lib. I. § 2. 'The princess was laid in the cradle of her boy-spouse,' and, says another, 'the infants embraced with smiles, from whence the bystanders drew a joyful omen of their future happiness.'

Ibid. 'If thou love him.' Cf. Lib. I. § 6. 'The Lord by His hidden inspiration, so inclined towards her the heart of the prince, that in the solitude of secret and mutual love he used to speak sweetly to her heart, with kindness and consolation: and was always wont, on returning home, to honour her with presents, and soothe her with embraces.' It was their custom, says Dietrich, to the last to call each other in common conversation, 'Brother,' and 'Sister.'

P. 35. 'To his charge.' Cf. Lib. I. § 7. 'Walter of Varila, a good man, who, having been sent by the prince's father into Hungary, had brought the blessed Elizabeth into Thuringen land.'

P. 37. 'The blind archer, Love.' For information about the pagan orientalism of the Troubadours, the blasphemous bombast by which they provoked their persecution in Provence, and their influence on the courts of Europe, *see* SISMONDI, *Lit. Southern Europe*, Cap. III.—VI.

P. 39. 'Stadings.' The Stadings, according to Fleury, in A D. 1233, were certain unruly fen-men, who refused to pay tithes, committed great cruelties on religious of both sexes, worshipped, or were said to worship, a black cat, &c., considered the devil as a very ill-used personage, and the rightful lord of themselves and the world, and were of the most profligate morals. An impartial and philosophic investigation of this and other early continental heresies, is much wanted.

P. 52. 'All gold.' Cf. Lib. I. § 7. For Walter's interference and Lewis's answer, which I have paraphrased.

P. 54. 'Is crowned with thorns.' Cf. Lib. I. § 5, for this anecdote and her defence, which I have in like manner paraphrased.

Ibid. 'Their pardon.' Cf. Lib. I. § 3, for this quaint method of self humiliation.

P. 55. 'You know your place.' Cf. Lib. I. § 6. 'The vassals and relations of her betrothed persecuted her openly, and plotted to send her back to her father divorced . . . . Sophia also did all she could to place her in a convent. . . . . She delighted in the company of maids and servants, so that Sophia used to say sneeringly to her, "You should have been counted among the slaves who drudge, and not among the princes who rule."'

P. 57. 'Childish laughter.' Cf. Lib. I. § 7. 'The holy maiden receiving the mirror, showed her joy by delighted laughter:' and again, II. § 8. 'They loved each other in the charity of the Lord, to a degree beyond all belief.'

Ibid. 'A crystal clear.' Cf. Lib. I. § 7.

P. 60. 'Our fairest bride.' Cf. Lib. I. § 8. 'No one henceforth dared oppose the marriage by word or plot,' . . . 'and all mouths were stopped.'

NOTES TO ACT II.

P. 62; p. 64; p. 65; p. 66. Cf. Lib. II. §§ 1, 5, 11, *et passim.*

Hitherto my notes have been a careful selection of the few grains of characteristic fact which I could find among Dietrich's lengthy professional reflections; but the chapter on which this scene is founded is remarkable enough to be given whole, and as I have a long-standing friendship for the good old monk, who is full of honest naïveté and deep-hearted sympathy, and have no wish to disgust *all* my readers with him, I shall give it for the most part untranslated. In the mean time, those who may be shocked at certain expressions in this poem, borrowed from the Romish devotional school, may verify my language at the Romish booksellers', who find just now a rapidly increasing sale for such ware. And is it not, after all, a hopeful sign for the age, that even the most questionable literary tastes must now-a-days ally themselves with religion—that the hotbed imaginations which used to batten on Rousseau and Byron, have now risen at least as high as the *Vies des Saints*, and St. Francois de Sales' Philothea? The truth is, that in such a time as this, in the dawn of an age of faith, whose future magnificence we may surely prognosticate from the slowness and complexity of its self-developing process, spiritual 'Werterism,' among other strange prolusions, must have its place. The emotions and the imaginations will assert their just right to be fed—by foul means, if not by fair; and even self-torture will have charms, after the utter dryness and life-in-death of mere ecclesiastical pedantry. It is good, mournful though it be, that a few, even by gorging themselves with poison, should indicate the rise of a spiritual hunger—if we do but take their fate as a warning to provide wholesome food before the new craving has extended itself to the many. It is good that religion should have its Werterism, in order that hereafter Werterism may have its religion. But to my quotations—wherein the reader will judge how difficult it has been for me to satisfy at once the delicacy of the English mind, and that historic truth which the highest art demands.

'Erat inter eos honorabile connubium, et thorus immaculatus, non in ardore libidinis, sed in conjugalis sanctimoniæ castitate. For the holy maiden, as soon as she was married, began to macerate her flesh with many watchings, rising every night to pray; her husband sometimes sleeping, sometimes conniving at her, often begging her, in compassion to her delicacy, not to afflict herself indiscreetly, often supporting her with his hand, when she prayed. ("And," says another of her biographers, "being taught by her to pray with her.") Great, truly, was the devotion of this young girl, who rising from the bed of her carnal husband, sought Christ, whom she loved as the *true husband of her soul.*

'Nor certainly was there less faith in the husband who did not oppose such and so great a wife, but rather favoured her, and tempered her fervour with over-kind prudence. Affected, therefore, by the sweetness of this modest love, and mutual society, they could not bear to be separated for any length of time or distance. The lady therefore frequently followed her husband through rough roads, and no small distances, and severe wind and weather, led rather by emotions of sincerity than of carnality: *for the chaste presence of a modest husband offered no obstacle to that devout spouse in the way of praying, watching, or otherwise doing good.*'

Then follows the story of her nurse waking Lewis instead of her, and Lewis's easy good-nature about this, as about every other event of life. 'And so, after these unwearied watchings, it often happened that praying for an excessive length of time, she fell asleep on a mat beside her husband's bed, and being reproved for it by her maidens, answered,—"Though I cannot always pray, yet I can do violence to my own flesh by tearing myself in the mean time from my couch."'

'Fugiebat oblectamenta carnalia, et ideò stratum molliorem, et *viri contubernium secretissimum, quantum licuit, declinavit. Quem quamvis præcordialis amoris affectu diligeret, querulabatur tamen dolens, quod virginalis decorem floris non meruit conservare.* Castigabat etiam plagis multis, et lacerabat diris verberibus carnem puella innocens et pudica.

'In principio quidem diebus quadragesimæ, sextisque feriis aliis occultas solebat accipere disciplinas, lætam coram, hominibus se ostentants. *Post verò convalescens et proficiens in gratia,* deserto dilecti thoro surgens, fecit se in secreto cubiculo per ancillarum manus gravi ter sæpissime verberari, ad lectumque mariti reversa hilarem se exhibuit et jocundam.

'Vere felices conjuges, in quorum consortio tanta munditia, in colloquio pudicitia reperta est. In quibus amor Christi concupiscentiam extinxit, devotio refrenavit petulantiam, fervor spiritûs excussit somnolentiam, oratio tutavit conscientiam, charitas benefaciendi facultatem tribuit et lætitiam!'

P. 79. 'In every scruple,' Cf. Lib. III. § 9, how Lewis 'consented that Elizabeth his wife should make a vow of obedience and continence at the will of the said Conrad, *salvâ jure matrimonii*.'

P. 81. 'The open street.' Cf. Lib. II. § 11. 'On the Rogation days, when certain persons doing contrary to the decrees of the saints are decorated with precious and luxurious garments, the Princess, dressed in serge and barefooted, used to follow most devoutly the Procession of the cross and the relics of the Saints, and place herself always at sermon among the poorest women, "knowing," says Dietrich, "that seeds cast into the valleys spring up into the richest crop of corn."'

Ibid. 'The poor of Christ.' Cf. Lib. II. §§ 6, 11, *et passim*. Elizabeth's labours among the poor are too well known throughout one half at least of Christendom, where she is, *par excellence*, the patron of the poor, to need quotations.

P. 83. 'I'll be thy pupil.' Cf. Lib. II. § 4. 'She used also, by words and examples, to oblige the worldly ladies who came to her to give up the vanity of the world, at least in some one particular.'

P. 85. 'Conrad enters.' Cf. Lib. III. § 9, where this story of the disobeyed message and the punishment inflicted by Conrad for it, is told word for word.

P. 89. 'Peaceably come by.' Cf. Lib. II. § 6.

P. 90. 'Bond slaves.' Cf. Note 11.

P. 93. 'Elizabeth passes.' Cf. Lib. II. § 5. 'This most Christian mother, impletis *purgationis suæ* diebus, used to dress herself in serge, and taking in her arms her new-born child, used to go forth secretly barefooted by the difficult descent from the castle by a rough and rocky road to a remote church, carrying her infant in her own arms, after the example of the Virgin Mother, and offering him upon the altar to the Lord with a taper,' (and with gold, says another biographer.)

P. 95. 'Give us bread.' Cf. Lib. III. § 6. 'A. D. 1225, while the Landgrave was gone to Italy to the Emperor, a severe famine arose throughout all Almaine; and lasting for nearly two years, destroyed many with hunger. Then Elizabeth, moved with compassion for the miserable, collected all the corn from her granaries, and distributed it as alms for the poor. She also built a hospital at the foot of the Wartburg, wherein she placed all those who could not wait for the general distribution. . . . . She sold her own ornaments to feed the members of Christ. . . . . Cuidam misero lac desideranti, ad mulgendum se præbuit!'—See p. 162.

P. 107. 'Ladies' tenderness.' Cf. Lib. III. § 8. 'When the courtiers and stewards complained on his return of the Lady Elizabeth's too great extravagance in alms-giving, "Let her alone," quoth he, "to do good, and to give whatever she will for God's sake, only keep Wartburg and Neuenburg in my hands." '

P. 116. 'A crusader's cross.' Cf. Lib. IV. § 1. 'In the year 1227 there was a general "Passagium" to the holy land, in which Frederick the Emperor also crossed the seas,' (or rather did *not* cross, says Heinrich Stero, in his annals, but having got as far as Sicily, came back again,—miserably disappointing and breaking up the expedition, whereof the greater part died at the various ports,—and was excommunicated for so doing;) 'and Lewis, landgrave of the Thuringians, took the cross likewise in the name of Jesus Christ, and. . . . . did not immediately fix the badge which he had received to his garment, as the manner is, lest his wife, who loved him with the most tender affection, seeing this, should be anxious and disturbed, ... but she found it while turning over his purse and fainted, struck down with a wonderful consternation.'

P. 120. 'I must be gone.' Cf. Lib. IV. § 2. A chapter in which Dietrich rises into a truly noble and pathetic strain. 'Coming to Schmalcald,' he says, 'Lewis found his dearest friends, whom he had ordered to meet him there, not wishing to depart without taking leave of them.'

Then follows Dietrich's only poetic attempt, which Basnage calls a '*carmen ineptum*, foolish ballad,' and most unfairly, as all readers should say, if I had any hope of doing justice in a translation to this genial fragment of an old dramatic ballad, and its simple objectivity, as of a writer so impressed (like all true Teutonic poets in those earnest days) with the pathos and greatness of his subject, that he never tries to 'improve' it by reflections, and preaching at his readers, but thinks it enough, just to tell his story, sure that it will speak for itself to all hearts.

Quibus valefaciens cum mœrore
Commisit suis fratribus natos cum uxore:
Matremque deosculatos filiali more,
Vix eam alloquitur cordis præ dolore,
Illis mota viscera, corda tremuerunt,
Dum alter *in alterius colla irruerunt,*
Expetentes oscula, quæ vix receperunt
Propter multitudines, quæ eos compresserunt.
Mater tenens filium, uxorque maritum,
In diversa pertrahunt, et tenent invitum,
Fratres cum militibus velut compeditum
Stringunt, nec discedere sinunt expeditum.
Erat in exercitu maximus tumultus,
Cum *carorum cernerent alternari vultus.*
Flebant omnes pariter, senex et adultus,
Turbæ cum militibus, cultus et incultus.
Eja! Quis non plangeret, cum videret flentes
Tot honestos nobiles, tam diversas gentes,
Cum Thuringis Saxones illuc venientes,
Ut viderent socios suos abscedentes.

Amico luctamine cuncti certavere,
Quis eum diutius posset retinere;
Quidam collo brachiis, *quidam inhæsere*
Vestibus, nec poterat cuiquam respondere.
Tandem *se de manibus eximens suorem*
Magnatorum socius et peregrinorum,
Admixtus tandem cœtui cruce signatorum
Non visurus amplius terram Thuringorum!

Surely there is a heart of flesh in the old monk which, when warmed by a really healthy subject, can toss aside Scripture-parodies, and professional Stoic-sentiment, and describe with such life and pathos, like any eye-witness, a scene which occurred, in fact, two years before his birth.

'And thus this *Prince of Peace*,' he continues, 'mounting his horse with many knights, &c. . . . . about the end of the month of June, set forth in the name of the Lord, praising him in heart and voice, and weeping and singing were heard side by side. And close by followed, with saddest heart, that most faithful lady after her sweetest prince, her most loving spouse, never, alas! to behold him more. And when she was going to return, the force of love and the agony of separation forced her on with him one day's journey; and yet that did not suffice. She went on, still unable to bear the parting, another full day's journey. . . . . At last they part, at the exhortations of Rudolf the Cupbearer. What groans, think you, what sobs, what struggles, what yearnings of the heart must there have been? Yet they part, and go on their way. . . . . The Lord went forth exulting, as a giant to run his course; the Lady returned lamenting, as a widow, and tears were on her cheeks. Then putting off the garments of joy, she took the dress of widowhood. The mistress of nations, sitting alone, she turned herself utterly to God—to her former good works, adding better ones.'

Their children were, 'Hermann, who became Landgraf; a daughter, who married the Duke of Brabant; another, who remaining in virginity, became a nun of Aldenburg, of which place she is lady abbess until this day.'

NOTES TO ACT III.

P. 125. 'On the freezing stone.' Cf. Lib. II. § 5. 'In the absence of her husband she used to lay aside her gay garments, conducted herself devoutly as a widow, and waited for the return of her beloved, passing her nights in watchings, genuflexions, prayers, and disciplines.' And again, Lib. IV. § 3, just quoted.

P. 127. 'The will of God.' Cf. Lib. IV. § 6. 'The mother-in-law said to her daughter-in-law, "Be brave, my beloved daughter; nor be disturbed at that which hath happened by divine ordinance to thy husband, my son." Whereto she answered boldly, "If my brother is captive, he can be freed by the help of God and our friends." "He is dead," quoth the other. Then she, clasping her hands upon her knees, "The world is dead to me, and all that is pleasant in the world." Having said this, suddenly springing up with tears, she rushed swiftly through the whole length of the palace, and being entirely beside herself, would have run on to the world's end, *usque quâque*, if a wall had not stopped her; and others coming up, led her away from the wall to which she had clung.'

P. 128. 'Yon lion's rage.' Cf. Lib. III. § 2. 'There was a certain lion in the court of the Prince; and it came to pass on a time, that rising from his bed in the morning, and crossing the court dressed only in his gown and slippers, he met this lion loose and raging against him. He thereon threatened the beast with his raised fist, and rated it manfully, till laying aside its fierceness, it lay down at the knight's feet, and fawned on him, wagging its tail.' So Dietrich.

P. 132; p. 138. Cf. Lib. IV. § 7.

'Now shortly after the news of Lewis's death, certain vassals of her late husband (with Henry, her brother-in-law,) cast her out of the castle and of all her possessions. . . . . . She took refuge that night in a certain tavern, ... and went at midnight to the matins of the "Minor Brothers." . . . . . And when no one dare give her lodging, took refuge in the church. . . . . . And when her little ones were brought to her from the castle, amid most bitter frost, she knew not where to lay their heads. . . . . . She entered a priest's house, and fed her family miserably enough, by pawning what she had. There was in that town an enemy of hers, having a roomy house. . . . . . Whither she entered at his bidding, and was forced to dwell with her whole family in a very narrow space, ... her host and hostess heaped her with annoyances and spite. She therefore bade them farewell, saying, "I would willingly thank mankind, if they would give me any reason for so doing." So she returned to her former filthy cell.'

P. 133. 'White as whales' bone,' (*i.e.* the tooth of the narwhal;) a common simile in the older poets.

P. 139. 'The nuns of Kitzingen.' Cf. Lib. V. § 1. 'After this, the noble Lady the Abbess of Kitzingen, Elizabeth's aunt according to the flesh, brought her away honourably to Eckembert, Lord Bishop of Bamberg.'

P. 141. 'Aged crone.' Cf. Lib. IV. where this whole story is related word for word.

P. 145. 'I'd mar this face.' Cf. Lib. V. § 1. 'If I could not,' said she, 'escape by any other means, I would with my own hands cut off my nose, that so every man might loath me when so foully disfigured.'

P. 147. 'Botenstain.' Cf. ibid. 'The Bishop commanded that she should be taken to Botenstain with her maids, until he should give her away in marriage.'

Ibid. 'Bear children.' Ibid. 'The venerable man, knowing that the apostle says, "I will that the younger widows marry, and bear children," thought of giving her in marriage to some one—an inten tion which she perceived. And protested on the strength of her "votum continentia." '

P. 150. 'The tented field.' All records of the worthy Bishop on which I have fallen, describe him as 'virum militiâ strenuissimum,' —a mighty man of war.—We read of him, in Stero of Altaich's Chronicle, A.D. 1232, making war on the Duke of Carinthia, destroying many of his castles, and laying waste a great part of his land; and next year, being seized by some bailiff of the Duke's, and keeping that Lent in durance vile. In A.D. 1237, he was left by the Emperor as 'vir magnanimus et bellicosus,' in charge of Austria, during the troubles with Duke Frederick; and died in 1240.

P. 152. 'Lewis's bones.' Cf. Lib. V. § 3.

P. 156. 'I thank thee.' Cf. Lib. V. § 4. 'What agony and love there was then in her heart, He alone can tell, who knows the hearts of all the sons of men. I believe that her grief was renewed, and all her bones trembled, when she saw the bones of her beloved separated one from another (the corpse had been dug up at Otranto, and *boiled*). But though absorbed in so great a woe, at last she remembered God, and recovering her spirit, said '—Her words I have paraphrased as closely as possible.)

P. 157. 'The close hard by.' Cf. Lib. V. § 4.

NOTES TO ACT IV.

P. 158. 'Your self-imposed vows.' Cf. Lib. IV. § 1. 'On Good Friday, when the altars were exhibited bare in remembrance of the Saviour who hung bare on the cross for us, she went into a certain chapel, and in the presence of Master Conrad, and certain Franciscan brothers, laying her holy hands on the bare altar, renounced her own will, her parents, children, relations, "Et omnibus hujus modi pompis," all pomps of this kind (a misprint, one hopes, for mundi), in imitation of Christ; and "omninò se exuit et nudavit," stripped herself utterly naked, to follow Him naked, in the steps of poverty.'

P. 162. 'All worldly goods.' A paraphrase of her own words.

P. 163. 'Thine own needs.' 'But when she was going to renounce her possessions also, the prudent Conrad stopped her.' The reflections which follow are Dietrich's own.

P. 164. 'The likeness of the fiend,' &c. I have put this daring expression into Conrad's mouth, as the ideal outcome of the teaching of Conrad's age on this point—and of much teaching also, which miscalls itself protestant, in our own age. The doctrine is not, of course, to be found *totidem verbis* in the formularies of any sect—yet almost all sects preach it, and quote Scripture for it as boldly as Conrad—the Romish Saint alone carries it honestly out into practice.

P. 166. 'With pine boughs.' Cf. Lib. VI. § 2. 'Entering a certain desolate court, she betook herself, "sub gradu cujusdam caminatæ," to the projection of a certain furnace, where she roofed herself in with boughs. . . . . In the mean time, in the town of Marpurg, was built for her a humble cottage of clay and timber.'

Ibid. 'Count Pama.' Cf. Lib. VI. § 6.

P. 168. 'Isentrudis and Guta.' Cf. Lib. VII. § 4. 'Now Conrad, as a prudent man, perceiving that this disciple of Christ wished to arrive at the highest pitch of perfection, studied to remove all which he thought would retard her, ... and therefore drove from her all those of her former household in whom she used to solace or delight herself. Thus the holy priest deprived this servant of God of all society, that so the constancy of her obedience might become known, and occasion might be given to her for clinging to God alone.'

P. 168. 'A leprous boy,' Cf. Lib. VI. § 8.
She had several of these protégés, successively, whose diseases are too disgusting to be specified, on whom she lavished the most menial cares. All the other stories of her benevolence which occur in these two pages are related by Dietrich.

P. 169. 'Mighty to save.' Cf. Lib. VII. § 7. Where we read, amongst other matters, how the objects of her prayers used to become while she was speaking so intensely *hot*, that they not only smoked, and nearly melted, but burnt the fingers of those who touched them: from whence Dietrich bids us 'learn with what an ardour of charity she used to burn, who would dry up with her heat the flow of worldly desire, and inflame to the love of eternity.'

P. 171. 'Lands and titles.' Cf. Lib. V. §§ 7, 8.

P. 172. 'Spinning wool.' Cf. Lib. VI. § 6. 'And crossing himself for wonder, the Count Pama cried out and said, "Was it ever seen to this day that a king's daughter should spin wool?" "All his messages from her father," says Dietrich, "were of no avail."'

P. 178. 'To do her penance.' Cf. Lib. VII. § 4. 'Now, he had placed with her certain austere women, from whom she endured much oppression patiently for Christ's sake, who, watching her rigidly, frequently reported her to her master for having transgressed her obedience, in giving something to the poor, or begging others to give. And when thus accused, she often received many blows from her master, insomuch that he used to strike her in the face, which she earnestly desired to endure patiently in memory of the stripes of the Lord.'

P. 180. 'That she dared not.' Cf. Lib. VII. § 4. 'When her most intimate friends, Isentrudis and Guta,' (whom another account describes as in great poverty,) 'came to see her, she dared not give them any thing, even for food, nor, without special license, salute them.'

Ibid. 'To bear within us.' 'Seeing in the church of certain monks who "professed poverty," images sumptuously gilt, she said to about twenty-four of them, "You had better to have spent this money on your own food and clothes, for we ought to have the reality of these images written in our hearts." And if any one mentioned a beautiful image before her, she used to say, "I have no need of such an image. I carry the thing itself in my bosom." '

P. 180. 'Even on her bed.' Cf. Lib. VI. §§ 5, 6.

P. 182. 'My mother rose.' Cf. Lib. VI. § 8. 'Her mother, who had been long ago' (when Elizabeth was nine years old) 'miserably slain by the Hungarians, appeared to her in her dreams upon her knees, and said, "My beloved child! pray for the agonies which I suffer; for thou canst." Elizabeth waking, prayed earnestly, and falling asleep again, her mother appeared to her and told her that she was freed, and that Elizabeth's prayers would hereafter benefit all who invoked her.' Of the causes of her mother's murder, the less that is said, the better—but the prudent letter which the Bishop of Gran sent back when asked to join in the conspiracy against her, is worthy notice. '*Reginam occidere nolite timere bonum est. Si omnes consentiunt ego non contradico.*' To be read as a full consent, or as a flat refusal, according to the success of the plot.

P. 184. 'Any living soul.' Dietrich has much on this point, headed, 'How master Conrad exercised Saint Elizabeth in the breaking of her own will. . . . . And at last forbad her entirely to give alms; whereon she employed herself in washing lepers and other infirm folk. In the mean time she was languishing, and inwardly tortured with emotions of compassion.'

I may here say, that in representing Elizabeth's early death as accelerated by a 'broken heart,' I have, I believe, told the truth, though I find no hint of any thing of the kind in Dietrich. The religious public of a petty town in the 13th century, round the death-bed of a royal saint, would of course treasure up most carefully all incidents connected with her latter days; but they would hardly record sentiments or expressions which might seem to their notions to derogate in any way from her saintship. Dietrich, too, looking at the subject as a monk and not as a man, would consider it just as much his duty to make her death-scene rapturous, as to make both her life and her tomb miraculous. I have composed these last scenes in the belief that Elizabeth and all her compeers will be recognized as real saints, in proportion as they are felt to have been real men and women.

P. 186. 'Eructate sweet doctrine.' The expressions are Dietrich's own.

Ibid. 'In her coffin yet.' Cf. Lib. VIII. § 1.

P. 187. 'So she said.' Cf. ibid.

Ibid. 'The poor of Christ.' 'She begged her master to distribute all to the poor, except a worthless tunic in which she wished to be buried. She made no will: she would have no heir besides Christ,' (i. e. the poor.)

P. 188. 'Martha and their brother,' &c.

I have compressed the events of several days into one in this scene. I give Dietrich's own account, omitting his reflections.

'When she had been ill twelve days and more, one of her maids sitting by her side, heard in her throat a very sweet sound, ... and saying, " Oh, my mistress, how sweetly thou didst sing!" she answered, "I tell thee, I heard a little bird between me and the wall sing merrily; who with his sweet song so stirred me up, that I could not but sing myself." '

Again, § 3. 'The last day she remained till evening most devout, having been made partaker of the celestial table, and inebriated with that most pure blood of life, which is Christ. The word of truth was continually on her lips, and opening her mouth of wisdom, she spake of the best things which she had heard in sermons; eructating from her heart good words, and the law of clemency was heard on her tongue. She told from the abundance of her heart how the Lord Jesus condescended to console Mary and Martha, at the raising again of their brother Lazarus, and then, speaking of His weeping with them over the dead, she eructated the memory of the abundance of the Lord's sweetness, affectu et effectu, (in feeling and expression?) Certain religious persons who were present, hearing these words, fired with devotion, by the grace which filled her lips, melted into tears. To whom the saint of God, now dying, recalled the sweet words of her Lord as he went to death, saying, "Daughters of Jerusalem," &c. Having said this she was silent. A wonderful thing. Then most sweet voices were heard in her throat, without any motion of her lips; and she asked of those round, "Did ye not hear some singing with me?" "Whereon none of the faithful are allowed to doubt," says Dietrich, "when she herself heard the harmony of the heavenly hosts, &c. &c." . . . . From that time to twilight she lay, as if exultant and jubilant, showing signs of remarkable devotion, till the crowing of the cock. Then, as if secure in the Lord, she said to the bystanders, "What should we do, if the fiend showed himself to us?" And shortly afterwards with a loud and clear voice, "Fly! fly!" as if repelling the dæmon.'

'At the cock-crow she said, "Here is the hour, in which the Virgin brought forth the child Jesus and laid him in a manger. . . . . Let us talk of him, and of that new star which he created by his omnipotence, which never before was seen." "For these," (says Montanus in her name,) "are the venerable mysteries of our faith, our richest blessings, our fairest ornaments: in these all the reason of our hope flourishes, faith grows, charity burns." '

The novelty of the style and matter will, I hope, excuse its prolixity with most readers. If not, I have still my reasons for inserting the greater part of this chapter.

P. 191. 'I demand it.' How far I am justified in putting such fears into her mouth, the reader may judge. Cf. Lib. VIII. § 5. 'The devotion of the people demanding it, her body was left unburied till the fourth day, in the midst of a multitude.' . . . .

'The flesh,' says Dietrich, 'had the tenderness of a living body, and was easily moved hither and thither, at the will of those who handled it. . . . . And many, sublime in the valour of their faith, tore off the hair of her head, and the nails of her fingers, ("even the tips of her ears, *et mamillarum papillas*," says untranslatably Montanus of Spire,) and kept them as relics.' The reference relating to the pictures of her disciplines, and the effect which they produced on the crowd, I have unfortunately lost.

P. 192. 'And yet no pain.' Cf. Lib. VIII. § 4. 'She said, "Though I am weak, I feel no disease or pain," and so through that whole day and night, as hath been said, having been elevated with most holy affections of mind towards God, and inflamed in spirit with most divine utterances and conversations, at length she rested from jubilating, and inclining her head as if falling into a sweet sleep, expired.'

NOTES TO ACT V.

P. 193. 'Canonization.' Cf. Lib. VIII. § 10. If I have in the last scene been guilty of a small anachronism, I have in this been guilty of a great one. Conrad was of course a prime means of Elizabeth's canonization, and, as Dietrich, and his own 'Letter to Pope Gregory the Ninth' show, collected, and pressed on the notice of the Archbishop of Maintz, the miraculous statements necessary for that honour. But he died two years before the actual publication of her canonization. It appeared to me, that by following the exact facts, I must either lose sight of the final triumph, which connects my heroine forever with Germany and all Romish Christendom, and is the very culmination of the whole story, or relinquish my only opportunity of doing Conrad justice, by exhibiting the remaining side of his character.

I am afraid that I have erred, and that the most strict historic truth would have coincided, as usual, with the highest artistic effect, while it would have only corroborated the moral of my poem, supposing that there is one. But I was fettered by the poverty of my own imagination, and 'do manus lectoribus.'

P. 194. 'Third Minors.' The order of the Third Minors of St. Francis of Assisi, was an invention of the comprehensive mind of that truly great man, by which 'worldlings' were enabled to participate in the spiritual advantages of the Franciscan rule and discipline, with out neglect or suspension of their civic and family duties. But it was an institution too enlightened for its age; and family and civic ties were destined for a far nobler consecration. The order was persecuted, and all but exterminated, by the jealousy of the Regular Monks, not, it seems, without papal connivance. Within a few years after its foundation it numbered amongst its members the noblest knights and ladies of Christendom, St. Louis of France among the number.

P. 195. 'Lest he fall.' Cf. Fleury *Eccl. Annals*, in Anno 1233. 'Doctor Conrad of Marpurg, the King Henry, son of the Emperor Frederick, &c., called an assembly at Mayence to examine persons accused as heretics. Among whom the Count of Saym demanded a delay to justify himself. As for the others who did not appear, Conrad gave the cross to those who would take up arms against them. At which these supposed heretics were so irritated, that on his return they lay in wait for him near Marpurg, and killed him with brother Gerard of the order of Minors, a holy man. Conrad was accused of precipitation in his judgments, and of having burned *trop légérement* under pretext of heresy, many noble and not noble, monks, nuns, burghers, and peasants. For he had them executed the same day that they were accused, without allowing any appeal.'

P. 197. 'The Kaiser.' Cf. Lib. VIII. § 12, for a list of the worthies present.

P. 198. 'A Zingar wizard.' Cf. Lib. I. § 1. The Magician's name was Klingsohr. He has been introduced by Novalis into his novel of *Heinrich Von Ofterdingen*, as present at the famous contest of the Minnesingers on the Wartburg. Here is Dietrich's account:—

'There were in those days in the Landgrave's court six knights, nobles, &c., &c., "cantilenarum confectores summi," song-wrights of the highest excellence,' (either one of them or Klingsohr himself, was the author of the Nibelungen-lied, and the Helden-buch.)

'Now there dwelt then in the parts of Hungary, in the land which is called the "Seven Castles," a certain rich nobleman, worth 3000 marks a year, a philosopher, practised from his youth in secular literature, but nevertheless learned in the sciences of Necromancy and Astronomy. This master Klingsohr was sent for by the Prince to judge between the songs of these knights aforesaid. Who, before he was introduced to the Landgrave, sitting one night in Eisenach, in the court of his lodging, looked very earnestly upon the stars; and being asked if he had perceived any secrets, "Know that this night is born a daughter to the King of Hungary, who shall be called Elizabeth, and shall be a saint, and shall be given to wife to the son of this prince; in the fame of whose sanctity all the earth shall exult and be exalted."

'See!—He who by Balaam the wizard foretold the mystery of his own incarnation, himself foretold by this wizard the name and birth of his fore-chosen handmaid Elizabeth.' (A comparison of which Basnage says, that he cannot deny it to be intolerable.) I am not bound to explain all strange stories, but considering who and whence Klingsohr was, and the fact that the treaty of espousals took place a few months afterwards, 'adhuc sugens ubera desponsata est!' it is not impossible that King Andrew and his sage vassal may have had some previous conversation on the destination of the unborn princess.

P. 199. 'A robe.' Cf. Lib. II. § 9, for this story; on which Dietrich observes, 'Thus did her Heavenly Father clothe his lily Elizabeth, as Solomon in all his glory could not do.'

Ibid. 'The incarnate Son.' This story is told, I think, by Surias, and has been introduced, with an illustration by a German artist of the highest note, into a modern prose biography of this saint. (I have omitted much more of the same kind.)

Ibid. 'Sainthood's palm.' Cf. Lib. VIII. §§ 7, 8, 9. 'While to declare the merits of his handmaid Elizabeth, in the place where her body rested, Almighty God was thus multiplying the badges of her virtues, (*i. e.* miracles,) two altars were built in her praise in that chapel, which while Siegfried, Archbishop of Mayence, was consecrating, as he had evidently been commanded in a vision, at the prayers of that devout man master Conrad, preacher of the word of God, the said preacher commanded all who had received any grace of healing from the merits of Elizabeth, to appear next day before the

Archbishop and faithfully prove their assertions by witnesses. . . . . Then the Most Holy Father, Pope Gregory the Ninth, having made diligent examination of the miracles transmitted to him, trusting at the same time to mature and prudent counsels, and the Holy Spirit's providence, above all, so ordaining, his clemency disposing, and his grace admonishing, decreed that the Blessed Elizabeth was to be written among the catalogue of the saints on earth, since in heaven she rejoices as written in the Book of Life." . . . . . .

Then follow four chapters, headed severally.

§ 9. 'Of the solemn canonization of the Blessed Elizabeth.'

§ 10. 'Of the translation of the Blessed Elizabeth, (and how the corpse when exposed diffused round a miraculous fragrance.')

§ 11. 'Of the desire of the people to see, embrace, and kiss (says Dietrich) those sacred bones, the organs of the Holy Spirit, from which flowed so many graces of sanctities.'

§ 12. 'Of the sublime persons who were present, and their oblations.'

§ 13. 'A consideration of the divine mercy about this matter.'

'Behold! she who despised the glory of the world, and refused the company of magnates, is magnificently honoured by the dignity of the Pontifical office, and the reverent care of Imperial Majesty. And she who, seeking the lowest place in this life, sat on the ground, slept in the dust, is now raised on high, by the hands of Kings and Princes. . . . . It transcends all heights of temporal glory, to have been made like the saints in glory. For all the rich among the people "vultum ejus deprecantur," (pray for the light of her countenance,) and kings and princes offer gifts, magnates adore her, and all nations serve her. Nor without reason, for "she sold all and gave to the poor," and counting all her substance for nothing, bought for herself this priceless pearl of eternity.' One would be sorry to believe that such utterly mean considerations of selfish vanity, expressing as they do an extreme respect for the very pomps and vanities which they praise the saints for despising, really went to the making of any saint, Romish or other.

§ 14. 'Of the sacred oil which flowed from the bones of Elizabeth.' I subjoin the 'Epilogus.'

'Moreover, even as the elect handmaid of God, the most blessed Elizabeth, had shone during her life with wonderful signs of her virtues, so since the day of her blessed departure up to the present time, she is resplendent through the various quarters of the world with illustrious prodigies of miracles, the Divine power glorifying her. For to the blind, dumb, deaf, and lame, dropsical, possessed, and leprous, shipwrecked, and captives, "ipsius meritis," as a reward for her holy deeds, remedies are conferred. Also, to all diseases, necessities, and dangers, assistance is given. And, moreover, by the many corpses, "*puta sedecim*," say sixteen, wonderfully raised to life by her self, becomes known to the faithful the magnificence of the virtues of the Most High glorifying His saint. To that Most High be glory and honour forever. Amen.'

So ends Dietrich's story. The reader has by this time, I hope, read enough to justify, in every sense, Conrad's 'A corpse or two was raised, they say, last week,' and much more of the funeral oration which I have put into his mouth.

P. 200. 'Gallant gentleman.' Cf. Lib. VIII. § 6.

P. 202. 'Took the crown.' Cf. Lib. VIII. § 12.

Ibid. The 'olive' and the 'pearl' are Dietrich's own figures. The others follow the method of scriptural interpretation, usual in the writers of that age.

P. 212. 'Domini canes,' 'The Lord's hounds,' a punning sobriquet of the Dominican inquisitors, in allusion to their profession.

P. 214. 'Folquet,' Bishop of Toulouse, who had been in early life a Troubadour, distinguished himself by his ferocity and perfidy in the crusade against the Albigenses and Troubadours, especially at the surrender of Toulouse, in company with his chief abettor, the infamous Simon de Montfort. He died A.D. 1231. *See* SISMONDI, *Lit. of Southern Europe*, Cap. VI.

MISCELLANEOUS POEMS.

MISCELLANEOUS POEMS.

THE SANDS OF DEE.

I.

"O Mary, go and call the cattle home,
And call the cattle home,
And call the cattle home
Across the sands of Dee;"
The western wind was wild and dank wi' foam,
And all alone went she.

II.

The western tide crept up along the sand,
And o'er and o'er the sand,
And round and round the sand,
As far as eye could see.
The rolling mist came down and hid the land—
And never home came she.

III.

"Oh!" is it weed, or fish, or floating hair—
A tress o' golden hair,
A drowned maiden's hair
Above the nets at sea?
Was never salmon yet that shone so fair
Among the stakes on Dee."

IV.

They rowed her in across the rolling foam,
The cruel crawling foam,
The cruel hungry foam
To her grave beside the sea:
But still the boatmen hear her call the cattle home
Across the sands of Dee!

THE THREE FISHERS.

Three fishers went sailing out into the West,
  Out into the West as the sun went down;
Each thought on the woman who loved him the best,
  And the children stood watching them out of the town;
For men must work, and women must weep,
And there 's little to earn, and many to keep,
    Though the harbour bar be moaning.

Three wives sat up in the light-house tower,
And they trimmed the lamps as the sun went down,
They looked at the squall, and they looked at the shower,
  And the night rack came rolling up ragged and brown!
But men must work, and women must weep,
Though storms be sudden, and waters deep,
    And the harbour bar be moaning.

Three corpses lay out on the shining sands
  In the morning gleam as the tide went down,
And the women are weeping and wringing their hands
  For those who will never come back to the town;
For men must work, and women must weep,
And the sooner it 's over, the sooner to sleep —
    And good-bye to the bar and its moaning.

WEARILY STRETCHES THE SAND.

* * * * * * * *

WEARILY stretches the sand to the surge, and the surge
to the cloudland;
Wearily onward I ride, watching the wild wave alone.
Not as of old, like Homeric Achilles, *κυδεϊ γαιων*,
Joyous knight-errant of God, thirsting for labour and
strife;
No more on magical steed borne free through the regions
of ether,
But, like the hack which I ride, selling my sinew for
gold.
Fruit-bearing autumn is gone; let the sad quiet winter
hang o'er me —
What were the spring to a soul laden with sorrow and
shame?
Green leaves would fret me with beauty; my heart has
no time to bepraise them;
Gray rock, bough, surge, cloud — these wake no yearn-
ing within,
Sing not, thou sky-lark above! even angels pass hushed
by the weeper!
Scream on, ye sea-fowl! my heart echoes your desolate cry.

Sweep the dry sand on, thou wild wind, to drift o'er the shell and the sea-weed;
Sea-weed and shell, like my dreams, swept down the pitiless tide.
Just is the wave which uptore us; 'tis nature's own law which condemns us;
Woe to the weak who, in pride, build on the faith of the sand!
Joy to the oak of the mountain, he trusts to the might of the rock-clefts;
Deeply he mines, and in peace feeds on the wealth of the stone.

* * * * * * * *

SAPPHO.

SHE lay among the myrtles on the cliff;
Above her glared the noon; beneath, the sea.
Upon the white horizon Atho's peak
Weltered in burning haze; all airs were dead;
The cicale slept among the tamarisk's hair;
The birds sat dumb and drooping. Far below
The lazy sea-weed glistened in the sun;
The lazy sea-fowl dried their steaming wings;
The lazy swell crept whispering up the ledge,
And sank again. Great Pan was laid to rest;
And Mother Earth watched by him as he slept,
And hushed her myriad children for awhile.
She lay among the myrtles on the cliff;
And sighed for sleep, for sleep that would not hear,
But left her tossing still; for night and day
A mighty hunger yearned within her heart,
Till all her veins ran fever, and her cheek,
Her long thin hands, and ivory-channel'd feet,
Were wasted with the wasting of her soul.
Then peevishly she flung her on her face,
And hid her eyeballs from the blinding glare,

And fingered at the grass, and tried to cool
Her crisp hot lips against the crisp hot sward:
And then she raised her head, and upward cast
Wild looks from homeless eyes, whose liquid light
Gleamed out between deep folds of blue-black hair,
As gleam twin lakes between the purple peaks
Of deep Parnassus, at the mournful moon.
Beside her lay her lyre. She snatched the shell,
And waked wild music from its silver strings;
Then tossed it sadly by.—"Ah, hush!" she cries,
"Dead offspring of the tortoise and the mine!
Why mock my discords with thine harmonies?
Although a thrice-Olympian lot be thine,
Only to echo back in every tone,
The moods of nobler natures than thine own."

A MYTH.

I.

A FLOATING, a floating
Across the sleeping sea,
All night I heard a singing bird
Upon the topmast tree.

II.

" Oh came you from the isles of Greece
Or from the banks of Seine ;
Or off some tree in forests free,
Which fringe the western main ? "

III.

" I came not off the old world
Nor yet from off the new —
But I am one of the birds of God
Which sing the whole night through."

IV.

" Oh sing and wake the dawning —
Oh whistle for the wind ;
The night is long, the current strong,
My boat it lags behind."

V.

" The current sweeps the old world,
The current sweeps the new ;
The wind will blow, the dawn will glow,
Ere thou hast sailed them through."

THE ANGLER'S QUESTIONS.

I CANNOT tell what you say, green leaves,
I cannot tell what you say:
But I know that there is a spirit in you,
And a word in you this day.

I cannot tell what you say, rosy rocks,
I cannot tell what you say:
But I know that there is a spirit in you,
And a word in you this day.

I cannot tell what you say, brown streams,
I cannot tell what you say:
But I know that in you too a spirit doth live,
And a word doth speak this day.

THE WORD'S ANSWER.

"OH green is the colour of faith and truth,
And rose the colour of love and youth,
And brown of the fruitful clay.
Sweet Earth is faithful, and fruitful, and young,
And her bridal day shall come ere long,
And you shall know what the rocks and the streams
And the whispering woodlands say."

THE DEAD CHURCH.

I.

WILD, wild wind, wilt thou never cease thy sighing?
Dark, dark night, wilt thou never wear away?
Cold, cold church, in thy death sleep lying,
Thy Lent is past, thy Passion here, but not thine Easter-
 day.

II.

Peace, faint heart, though the night be dark and sigh-
 ing;
Rest, fair corpse, where thy Lord himself hath lain;
Weep, dear Lord, where thy bride is lying;
Thy tears shall wake her frozen limbs to life and health
 again.

A PARABLE FROM LIEBIG.

I.

THE church bells were ringing, the devil sat singing
On the stump of a rotting old tree;
" Oh faith, it grows cold, and the creeds they grow old,
And the world is nigh ready for me."

II.

The bells went on ringing, a spirit came singing,
And smiled as he crumbled the tree;
" Yon wood does but perish new seedlings to cherish,
And the world is to live yet for thee."

THERE SITS A BIRD.

THERE sits a bird on every tree,
With a heigh-ho!
There sits a bird on every tree,
Sings to his love, as I to thee,
With a heigh-ho, and a heigh-ho!
Young maids must marry.

There grows a flower on every bough,
With a heigh-ho!
There grows a flower on every bough,
Its gay leaves kiss—I'll show you how:
With a heigh-ho, and a heigh-ho!
Young maids must marry.

The sun 's a bridegroom, earth a bride;
With a heigh-ho!
The sun 's a bridegroom, earth a bride;
They court from morn to eventide:
The earth shall pass, but love abide.
With a heigh-ho, and a heigh-ho!
Young maids must marry.

TWIN STARS ALOFT.

Twin stars, aloft in ether clear,
Around each other roll alway,
Within one common atmosphere
Of their own mutual light and day.

And myriad happy eyes are bent
Upon their changeless love alway;
As strengthened by their one intent,
They pour the flood of life and day.

So we through this world's waning night,
Shall, hand in hand, pursue our way;
Shed round us order, love, and light,
And shine unto the perfect day.

YOUNG MARY.

YOUNG Mary walked sadly down through the green clover,
And sighed as she looked at the babe at her breast;
" My roses are faded, my false love a rover,
The green graves they call me, 'Come home to your rest.' "

Then by rode a soldier in gorgeous arraying,
And "where is your bride-ring, my fair maid!" he cried;
"I ne'er had a bride-ring, by false man's betraying,
Nor token of love but this babe at my side.

"Tho' gold could not buy me, sweet words could deceive me;
So faithful and lonely till death I must roam."
"O Mary, sweet Mary, look up and forgive me,
With wealth and with glory your true love comes home.

"So give my own babe, those soft arms adorning,
I'll wed you and cherish you, never to stray;
For it 's many a dark and a wild cloudy morning
Turns out by the noon-time a sunshiny day."

THE MERRY LARK WAS UP AND SINGING.

The merry, merry lark was up and singing,
  And the hare was out and feeding on the lea,
And the merry, merry bells below were ringing,
  When my child's laugh rang through me.
Now the hare is snared and dead beside the snow-yard,
  And the lark beside the dreary winter sea,
And my baby in his cradle in the churchyard
  Waiteth there until the bells bring me.

EPICEDIUM ON THE DEATH OF A CERTAIN JOURNAL.

So die, thou child of stormy dawn,
Thou winter flower, forlorn of nurse;
Chilled early by the bigot's curse,
The pedant's frown, the worldling's yawn.

Fair death, to fall in teeming June,
When every seed which drops to earth
Takes root, and wins a second birth
From steaming shower and gleaming moon.
Fall warm, fall fast, thou mellow rain;
Thou rain of God, make fat the land;
That roots which parch in burning sand
May bud to flower and fruit again.

To grace, perchance, a fairer morn
In mightier lands beyond the sea,
While honour falls to such as we
From hearts of heroes yet unborn.

Who in the blaze of riper day
Of purer science, holier laws,
Bless us, faint heralds of their cause,
Dim beacons of their glorious way.

Failure? While tide-floods rise and boil
Round cape and isle, in port and cove,
Resistless, star-led from above:
What though our tiny wave recoil?

A CHRISTMAS CAROL.

It chanced upon the merry, merry Christmas eve
  I went sighing past the church, across the moorland dreary—
"Oh! never sin and want and woe this earth will leave,
  And the bells but mock the wailing round, they sing so cheery.
How long, O Lord! how long before Thou come again?
  Still in cellar, and in garret, and on moorland dreary
The orphans moan, and widows weep, and poor men toil in vain,
  Till the earth is sick of hope deferred, though Christmas bells be cheery."

Then arose a joyous clamour from the wild fowl on the mere,
  Beneath the stars, across the snow, like clear bells ringing,
And a voice within cried—"Listen!—Christmas carols even here!
  Though thou be dumb, yet o'er their work the stars and snows are singing.

Blind! I live, I love, I reign; and all the nations through
With the thunder of my judgments even now are ringing;
Do thou fulfil thy work, but as yon wild fowl do,
Thou wilt heed no less the wailing yet hear through it angels' singing."

MY HUNTING SONG.

FORWARD ! hark ! forward 's the cry !
One more fence and we 're out on the open !
So to us at once, if you want to live near us—
Follow them, hark to them, darlings ! as on they go,
Leaping and sweeping down into the vale below !
Cowards and bunglers whose heart or whose eye is slow
Find themselves staring alone.

So the great cause flashes by,
Nearer and clearer its purposes open,
While louder and louder the world-echoes cheer us :
Gentlemen, sportsmen, you *ought* to live up to us,
Lift us and lead us, and hallo our game to us—
We cannot take the hounds off, and no shame to us—
Don't be left staring alone !

SONGS.

Ask if I love thee? Oh smiles cannot tell
Plainer what tears are now showing too well.
Had I not loved thee, my sky had been clear:
Had I not loved thee, I had not been here,
Weeping for thee!

Ask if I love thee? How else could I borrow
Pride from man's calumny, strength from thy sorrow?
Laugh when they sneer at the fanatic's bride
Knowing no bliss, save to toil and to bide
Weeping for thee!

II.

The world goes up and the world goes down,
And the sunshine follows the rain;
And yesterday's sneer and yesterday's frown
Can never come over again,
Sweet wife,
No, never come over again.

For woman is warm though man be cold,
And the night will hallow the day;
Till the heart which at even was weary and old
Can rise in the morning gay,
Sweet wife,
To its work in the morning gay.

THE UGLY PRINCESS.

I.

My parents bow and lead them forth
  For all the crowd to see—
Ah well! the people might not care
  To cheer a dwarf like me.

II.

They little know how I could love,
  How I could plan and toil,
To swell those drudges' scanty gains,
  Their mites of rye and oil.

III.

They little know what dreams have been
  My playmates, night and day;
Of equal kindness, helpful care,
  A mother's perfect sway.

IV.

Now earth to earth in convent walls,
  To earth in churchyard sod:
I was not good enough for man,
  And so am given to God.

A THOUGHT FROM THE RHINE.

I HEARD an Eagle crying all alone
Above the vineyards through the summer night,
Among the skeletons of robber towers,—
The iron homes of iron-hearted lords,
Now crumbling back to ruin year by year,—
Because the ancient eyrie of his race
Is trenched and walled by busy-handed men,
And all his forest-chace and woodland wild,
Wherefrom he fed his young with hare and roe,
Are trim with grapes, which swell from hour to hour
And toss their golden tendrils to the sun
For joy at their own riches :—So, I thought,
The great devourers of the earth shall sit,
Idle and impotent, they know not why,
Down-staring from their barren height of state
On nations grown too wise to slay and slave,
The puppets of the few, while peaceful love
And fellow-help make glad the heart of earth,
With wonders which they fear and hate, as he
The Eagle hates the vineyard slopes below.

SONNET.

The baby sings not on its mother's breast—
Nor nightingales who nestle side by side—
Nor I by thine: but let us only part,
Then lips which should but kiss and so be still,
As having uttered all, must speak again.—
Oh stunted thoughts! Oh chill and fettered rhyme!
Yet my great bliss, though still entirely blest,
Losing its proper home can find no rest:
So—like a child who whiles away the time
With dance and carol till the eventide,
Watching its mother homeward through the glen;
Or nightingale, who sitting far apart,
Tells to his listening mate within the nest
The wonder of his star-entranced heart
Till all the wakened woodlands laugh and thrill—
Forth all my being bubbles into song,
And rings aloft, not smooth, yet clear and strong.

BALLADS.

BALLADS.

A. D. 415.

OVER the camp-fires
Drank I with heroes,
Under the Donau bank
Warm in the snow-trench:
Sagamen heard I there,
Men of the Longbeards,
Cunning and ancient,
Honey-sweet-voiced.
Scaring the wolf cub,
Scaring the horn-owl out,
Shaking the snow-wreaths
Down from the pine-boughs,
Up to the star-roof
Rang out their song.
Singing how Winil men,
Over the ice-floes
Sledging from Scanland on
Came unto Scoring ;
Singing of Gambara

Freya's beloved,
Mother of Ayo,
Mother of Ibor.
Singing of Wendel men,
Ambri and Assi;
How to the Winilfolk
Went they with war-words,—
"Few are ye, strangers,
And many are we;
Pay us now toll and fee,
Clothyarn, and rings, and beeves;
Else at the raven's meal
Bide the sharp bill's doom."

Clutching the dwarf's work, then,
Clutching the bullock's shell,
Girding gray iron on,
Forth fared the Winils all,
Fared the Alruna's sons,
Ayo and Ibor.
Mad of heart stalked they:
Loud wept the women all,
Loud wept the Alruna wife;
Sore was their need.

Out of the morning land,
Over the snow-drifts,
Beautiful Freya came,
Tripping to Scoring.

White were the moorlands
And frozen before her;
But green were the moorlands,
And blooming behind her,
Out of her golden locks
Shaking the spring flowers,
Out of her garments
Shaking the south wind,
Around in the birches
Awaking the throstles,
And making chaste housewives all
Long for their heroes home,
Loving and love-giving,
Came she to Scoring.
Came unto Gambara,
Wisest of Valas,—
"Vala, why weepest thou?
Far in the wide-blue,
High up in the Elfin-home,
Heard I thy weeping."

"Stop not my weeping,
Till one can fight seven.
Sons have I, heroes tall,
First in the sword-play;
This day at the Wendels' hands
Eagles must tear them;
While their mothers, thrall-weary
Must grind for the Wendels."

Wept the Alruna wife;
Kissed her fair Freya: —
"Far off in the morning land,
High in Valhalla,
A window stands open
Its sill is the snow-peaks,
Its posts are the water-spouts,
Storm-rack its lintel;
Gold cloud-flakes above it
Are piled for the roofing.
Far up to the Elfin-home,
High in the wide-blue.
Smiles out each morning thence
Odin Allfather;
From under the cloud-eaves
Smiles out on the heroes,
Smiles out on chaste housewives all,
Smiles on the brood-mares,
Smiles on the smiths' work:
And theirs is the sword-luck,
With them is the glory,—
So Odin hath sworn it,—
Who first in the morning
Shall meet him and greet him."
Still the Alruna wept: —
"Who then shall greet him?
Women alone are here:
Far on the moorlands
Behind the war-lindens,

In vain for the bill's doom
Watch Winil heroes all,
One against seven."
Sweetly the Queen laughed: —
" Hear thou my counsel now;
Take to thee cunning,
Beloved of Freya.
Take thou thy women-folk,
Maidens and wives:
Over your ankles
Lace on the white war-hose;
Over your bosoms
Link up the hard mail-nets;
Over your lips
Plait long tresses with cunning; —
So war-beasts full-bearded
King Odin shall deem you,
When off the gray sea-beach
At sunrise ye greet him."

Night's son was driving
His golden-haired horses up;
Over the eastern firths
High flashed their manes.
Smiled from the cloud-eaves out
Allfather Odin,
Waiting the battle-sport:
Freya stood by him.

"Who are these heroes tall,—
Lusty-limbed Longbeards?
Over the swans' bath
Why cry they to me?
Bones should be crashing fast,
Wolves should be full-fed,
Where'er such, mad-hearted,
Swing hands in the sword-play."

Sweetly laughed Freya:—
"A name thou hast given them
Shames neither thee nor them,
Well can they wear it.
Give them the victory,
First have they greeted thee;
Give them the victory.
Yokefellow mine!
Maidens and wives are these,—
Wives of the Winils;
Few are their heroes
And far on the war-road,
So over the swans' bath
They cry unto thee."

Royally laughed he then;
Dear was that craft to him,
Odin Allfather,
Shaking the clouds.

"Cunning are women all,
Bold and importunate!
Longbeards their name shall be,
Ravens shall thank them:
Where the women are heroes,
What must the men be like?
Theirs is the victory;
No need of me!" *

* This punning legend may be seen in Paul Warnefrid's *Gesta Langobardorum.* Unfortunately, however, for the story, Lângbardr is said by the learned to have nothing to do with beards at all, but probably to mean "Longswords." The metre and language are intended as imitations of those of the earlier Eddaic poems.

A. D. 1100.

Evil sped the battle play
On the Pope Calixtus' day,
Mighty war-smiths, thanes and lords,
In Sangelac slept the sleep of swords,
Harold Earl shot over shield,
Lay along the autumn weald;
Slaughter such was never none
Since the Ethelings England won.
Thither Lady Githa came,
Weeping sore for grief and shame,
How may she her first-born tell?
Frenchmen stript him where he fell,
Gashed and marred his comely face,
Who can know him in his place?
Up and spake two brethren wise,
"Youngest hearts have keenest eyes;
Bird which leaves its mother's nest,
Moults its pinion, moults its crest.
Let us call the Swan-neck here,
She that was his lemman dear,
She shall know him in his stound;
Foot of colt, and scent of hound,
Eye of hawk, and wing of dove,
Carry woman to her love."

Up and spake the Swan-neck high,
"Go! to all your thanes, let cry
How I loved him best of all,
I whom men his lemman call;
Better knew his body fair
Than the mother, which him bare.
When ye lived in health and glee
Then ye scorned to look on me;
God hath brought the proud ones low
After me afoot to go."
Rousing erne, and sallow glede,
Rousing gray-wolf off his feed,
Over franklin, earl, and thane,
Heaps of mother-naked slain;
Round the red field tracing slow,
Stooped that swan-neck white as snow;
Never blushed, nor turned away,
Till she found him where he lay.
Clipt him in her armés fair,
Wrapt him in her yellow hair,
Bore him from the battle-stead,
Saw him laid in pall of lead,
Took her to a minster high,
For Earl Harold's soul to cry.

Thus fell Harold, bracelet-giver;
Jesu rest his soul forever;
Angels all from thrall deliver;
Miserere Domine.

A. D. 1400.

I.

It was Earl Haldan's daughter
She look'd across the sea;
She look'd across the water,
And long and loud laugh'd she:
"The locks of six princesses
Must be my marriage-fee,
So hey bonny boat, and ho bonny boat!
Who comes a-wooing me!"

II.

It was Earl Haldan's daughter,
She walked along the sand;
When she was aware of a knight so fair,
Come sailing to the land.
His sails were all of velvet,
His mast of beaten gold,
And "hey bonny boat, and ho bonny boat,
Who saileth here so bold?"

III.

"The locks of five princesses
I won beyond the sea;
I shore their golden tresses,
To fringe a cloak for thee.

One handfull yet is wanting,
But one of all the tale;
So hey bonny boat, and ho bonny boat!
Furl up thy velvet sail!"

IV.

He leapt into the water,
That rover young and bold;
He gript Earl Haldan's daughter,
He shore her locks of gold;
"Go weep, go weep, proud maiden,
The tale is full to-day.
Now hey bonny boat, and ho bonny boat!
Sail Westward ho, and away!"

A. D. 1500.

Oh, I wadna be a yeoman, mither, to follow my father's trade,
To bow my back in miry fallows, over plow and hoe and spade.
Stinting wife, and bairns, and kye, to fat some courtier lord,—
Let them die o' rent wha like, mither, and I'll die by sword.

Nor I wadna be a clerk, mither, to bide aye ben,
Scrabbling over sheets o' parchment with a weery, weery pen,
Looking through the lang stane windows at a narrow strip o' sky,
Like a laverock in a withy cage, until I pine away and die.
Nor I wadna be a merchant, mither, in his lang furred gown,
Trailing strings o' footsore horses through the noisy dusty town;
Louting low to knights and ladies, fumbling o'er his wares,
Telling lies, and scraping siller, heaping cares on cares.

Nor I wadna be a soldier, mither, to dice wi' ruffian bands,
Pining weery months in castles, looking over wasted lands,
Smoking byres, and shrieking women, and the grewsome sights o' war—
There 's blood on my hand enough, mither; it's ill to make it mair.

If I had married a wife, mither, I might ha' been douce and still,
And sat at hame by the ingle side to crack and laugh my fill;
Sat at hame wi' the woman I looed, and bairnies at my knee,
But death is bauld, and age is cauld, and luve's no for me.

For when first I stirred in your side, mither, ye ken full well
How you lay all night up among the deer on the open fell;
And so it was that I got the heart to wander far and neer,
Caring neither for land nor lassie, but the bonny dun deer.

Yet I am not a losel and idle, mither, nor a thief that steals;
I do but hunt God's cattle, upon God's ain hills;
For no man buys and sells the deer, and the fells are free

To a knight that carries hawk and spurs, and a hind
like me.

So I'm aff and away to the muirs, mither, to hunt the
deer;
Ranging far fra frowning faces, and the douce folk here;
Crawling up through burn and bracken, louping madly
down the screes,
Speering out fra' craig and headland, drinking up the
Simmer breeze.

Oh, the wafts o' heather honey, and the music o' the brae,
As I watch the great harts feeding, nearer, nearer a' the
day!
Oh, to hark the eagle screaming, sweeping, ringing round
the sky! —
That 's a bonnier life than stumbling owr'e the muck to
hog and kye.

And when I'm taen and hangit, mither, a brittling o' my
deer,
Ye'll no leave your bairn to the corbie craws to dangle
in the air;
But ye'll send up my twa douce brethren, and ye'll steal
me fra the tree,
And bury me up on the brown, brown muirs, where I
aye loved to be.

Ye'll bury me 'twixt the brae and the burn, in a glen far
away,

Where I may hear the heathcock craw, and the great harts bray;
And if my ghaist can walk, mither, I'll sit glowering at the sky,
The live long night on the black hill sides where the dun deer lie.

A. D. 1580.

Ah tyrant Love, Megæra's serpents bearing,
  Why thus requite my sighs with venom'd smart?
Ah, ruthless dove, the vulture's talons wearing,
  Why flesh them, traitress, in this faithful heart?
Is this my meed? Must dragon's teeth alone
  In Venus' lawns by lovers' hands be sown?
Nay, gentlest Cupid; 'twas my pride unbid me;
  Nay, guiltless dove; by mine own wound I fell.
To worship, not to wed, Celestials bid me:
  I dreamt to mate in heaven, and wake in hell;
Forever doom'd, Ixion-like, to reel
  On mine own passions' ever-burning wheel.

A. D. 1740.

I.

Oh England is a pleasant place for them that's rich and
high;
But England is a cruel place for such poor folks as I;
And such a port for mariners I ne'er shall see again,
As the pleasant Isle of Avès, beside the Spanish main.

II.

There were forty craft in Avès that were both swift and
stout,
All furnished well with small arms and cannons round
about;
And a thousand men in Avès made laws so fair and free
To choose their valiant captains and obey them loyally.

III.

Thence we sailed against the Spaniard with his hoards
of plate and gold,
Which he wrung by cruel tortures from the Indian folk
of old;
Likewise the merchant captains, with hearts as hard as
stone,
Which flog men and keel-haul them and starve them to
the bone.

IV.

Oh the palms grew high in Avès and fruits that shone
like gold,
And the colibris and parrots they were gorgeous to
behold;
And the negro maids to Avès from bondage fast did
flee,
To welcome gallant sailors a sweeping in from sea.

V.

Oh sweet it was in Avès to hear the landward breeze
A-swing with good tobacco in a net between the trees,
With a negro lass to fan you while you listened to the
roar
Of the breakers on the reef outside that never touched
the shore.

VI.

But Scripture saith, an ending to all fine things must be,
So the King's ships sailed on Avès and quite put down
were we.
All day we fought like bulldogs, but they burst the booms
at night;
And I fled in a piragua sore wounded from the fight.

VII.

Nine days I floated starving, and a negro lass beside,
Till for all I tried to cheer her, the poor young thing she
died;
But as I lay a gasping a Bristol sail came by,
And brought me home to England here to beg until I die.

VIII.

And now I'm old and going I'm sure I can't tell where;
One comfort is this world 's so hard I can't be worse off
there:
If I might but be a sea-dove I'd fly across the main,
To the pleasant Isle of Avès, to look at it once again.

A. D. 1848.

The merry brown hares came leaping
  Over the crest of the hill,
Where the clover and corn lay sleeping
  Under the moonlight still.

Leaping late and early,
  Till under their bite and their tread
The swedes, and the wheat, and the barley,
  Lay cankered, and trampled and dead.

A poacher's widow sat sighing
  On the side of the white chalk bank,
Where under the gloomy fir-woods
  One spot in the ley throve rank.

She watched a long tuft of clover,
  Where rabbit or hare never ran ;
For its black sour haulm covered over
  The blood of a murdered man

She thought of the dark plantation,
  And the hares, and her husband's blood,
And the voice of her indignation
  Rose up to the throne of God.

"I am long past wailing and whining—
  I have wept too much in my life:
I've had twenty years of pining
  As an English labourer's wife.

A labourer in Christian England,
  Where they cant of a Saviour's name,
And yet waste men's lives like the vermin's
  For a few more brace of game.

There 's blood on your new foreign shrubs, squire,
  There 's blood on your pointers' feet;
There 's blood on the game you sell, squire,
  And there 's blood on the game you eat.

You have sold the labouring-man, squire,
  Body and soul to shame,
To pay for your seat in the House, squire,
  And to pay for the feed of your game.

You made him a poacher yourself, squire,
  When you'd give neither work nor meat,
And your barley-fed hares robbed the garden
  At our starving children's feet;

When packed in one reeking chamber,
Man, maid, mother, and little ones lay;
While the rain pattered in on the rotting bride-bed,
And the walls let in the day;

When we lay in the burning fever
On the mud of the cold clay floor,
Till you parted us all for three months, squire,
At the cursed workhouse-door.

We quarrelled like brutes, and who wonders?
What self-respect could we keep,
Worse housed than your hacks and your pointers,
Worse fed than your hogs and your sheep?

Our daughters with base-born babies
Have wandered away in their shame;
If your misses had slept, squire, where they did,
Your misses might do the same.

Can your lady patch hearts that are breaking
With handfuls of coals and rice,
Or by dealing out flannel and sheeting
A little below cost price?

You may tire of the jail and the workhouse,
And take to allotments and schools,
But you 've run up a debt that will never
Be repaid us by penny-club rules.

In the season of shame and sadness,
  In the dark and dreary day,
When scrofula, gout, and madness,
  Are eating your race away;

When to kennels and liveried varlets
  You have cast your daughters' bread,
And, worn out with liquor and harlots,
  Your heir at your feet lies dead;

When your youngest, the mealy-mouthed rector,
  Lets your soul rot asleep to the grave,
You will find in your God the protector
  Of the freeman you fancied your slave."

She looked at the tuft of clover,
  And wept till her heart grew light;
And at last when her passion was over,
  Went wandering into the night.

But the merry brown hares came leaping
  Over the uplands still,
Where the clover and corn lay sleeping
  On the side of the white chalk hill.

PEOPLE'S SONG, 1849.

I.

Weep, weep, weep and weep,
For pauper, dolt, and slave!
Hark from wasted moor and fen,
Feverous alley, workhouse den,
Swells the wail of Saxon men—
Work! or the grave!

II.

Down, down, down and down
With idler, knave, and tyrant!
Why for sluggards cark and moil?
He that will not live by toil
Has no right on English soil!
God's word our warrant!

III.

Up, up, up and up!
Face your game and play it!
The night is past, behold the sun!—
The idols fall, the lie is done—
The Judge is set, the doom begun!
Who shall stay it?

THE DAY OF THE LORD.

The Day of the Lord is at hand, at hand!
Its storms roll up the sky:
A nation sleeps starving on heaps of gold;
All dreamers toss and sigh;
The night is darkest before the dawn—
When the pain is sorest the child is born,
And the Day of the Lord at hand.

Gather you, gather you, angels of God—
Freedom, and Mercy, and Truth;
Come! for the Earth is grown coward and old—
Come down and renew us her youth.
Wisdom, Self-sacrifice, Daring, and Love,
Haste to the battle-field, stoop from above,
To the Day of the Lord at hand.

Gather you, gather you, hounds of hell—
Famine, and Plague, and War;
Idleness, Bigotry, Cant, and Misrule,
Gather, and fall in the snare!
Hirelings and Mammonites, Pedants and Knaves,
Crawl to the battle-field—sneak to your graves,
In the Day of the Lord at hand.

Who would sit down and sigh for a lost age of gold,
  While the Lord of all ages is here?
True hearts will leap up at the trumpet of God,
  And those who can suffer, can dare.
Each old age of gold was an iron age too,
And the meekest of saints may find stern work to do,
      In the Day of the Lord at hand.